FASHIONABLE FOLKS

BONNETS AND HATS 1840-1900

FASHIONABLE FOLKS

BONNETS AND HATS 1840-1900

MAUREEN A. TAYLOR

Fashionable Folks: Bonnets and Hats 1840-1900

All images, unless indicated otherwise, are courtesy of the author's collection.

Published by Picture Perfect Press
www.PicturePerfectPress.com

ISBN 978-0-984-84500-2

Book and cover design by Anne L. Rolland

Printed in USA

To my Mom for suggesting I write about hats
and for Anita, who is never without one.

CONTENTS

ACKNOWLEDGMENTS

There are always so many people to thank at the end of a book project. This one is no different.

First and foremost thank you to the readers of my blogs—my personal blog [www.maureentaylor.com] and the Photo Detective blog at the Family Tree Magazine website [blog.familytreemagazine.com/photodetectiveblog/] -- the followers of my videos [Vimeo.com/photodetective] and all the subscribers to my free e-newsletter. Each time I've mentioned working on this project, pictures poured into my inbox.

Many people sent me pictures of their ancestors wearing twentieth-century hats but unfortunately I didn't include them here because I'm focusing on the nineteenth century. I'm hoping to use them in a future project, though. The contributors to this volume are: Maridee Alexander, Jean Sebasta, Elizabeth Handler, and Sandy Willis.

I frequently go to photo shows to buy images to use in books and projects. At each of these shows, I stop to chat with dealers, Greg French who maintains the site [www.gregfrenchearlyphotography.com], Erin Waters, and Sabine Ocker. Many of the images included here I've bought at their booths. Sabine's husband, Phil Storey, collects images of men in hats. When I mentioned I was working on this book, he sent me images. Thank you, Phil! The hats in your pictures helped me build this story of nineteenth-century millinery.

My good friend, Jane Schwerdtfeger, accompanies me on these photo buying trips. A couple of years ago, she let me scan all of the pictures in her collection. She has an amazing eye for spotting beautiful photos. No book would be complete without a selection from her collection.

I'm crazy about old photos and so is the author of the Shades of the Departed blog [www.shadesofthedeparted.com/]. The Footnote Maven writes a fantastic blog and edits an online magazine, Shades (through the same web link). She contributed two images to this volume—a great picture of a hat shop and one of an advertisement for hats.

The Library of Congress [www.loc.gov] has an incredible photo collection. You'll see many images from this collection in these pages. There are a couple of images here from the Medway Historical Society. Thank you to Marian Pierre-Louis of Fieldstone Historical Research [www.fieldstonehistoric] for introducing me to their collection.

I love historic newspapers as much as I do photographs. The pages of these old newspapers allow me to time travel without leaving my desk. I've been a long-time subscriber to GenealogyBank [www.genealogybank.com]. Thank you, Tom, for letting me share articles with my readers.

Thank to Kathy Crosett for careful copyediting and to Anne Rolland for a beautiful design.

I hope I haven't forgotten anyone…

INTRODUCTION

It appears that hats are back. Designer Philip Treacy's amazing hats for the rich and famous (including members of the Royal Family) stand out in the crowd. Small hats for men appear in television programs and new styles are showing up in shops for men and women who want to be fashion-forward. Musicians like Lady Gaga and Gwen Stefani, actor Brad Pitt, and television character Evan R. Lawson (Paulo Costanzo), on the hit show *Royal Pains*, are rarely without hats. After decades of decline, toppers grace the heads of stylish students. There are church going hats, as well as the Red Hat Club for women of a certain age.

It's appropriate with this revived passion for hats to look back on the toppers worn by our ancestors. At the end of the nineteenth century, a newspaper journalist wrote an opinion piece that asked "Why wear Hats?"[1] Hopefully, after looking at all the hats in this book, you'll have an answer.

I started talking about hats nearly two years ago. Since then, many people have told me about their own family history connection to the millinery industry. One man mentioned his grandmother raised the small birds that were stuffed for early twentieth-century hats; another told me about an ancestor who made hats for private clients. Through family history research, I discovered a personal connection to the hat industry. Some of my relatives who lived in Manchester, England in the 1840s were hatters. You can find out if your ancestor worked in the millinery business by checking census records, city directories, and tax lists.

In the nineteenth century, every season—spring, summer, fall, and winter—was awash in hats. There were hundreds of choices.

Contemporary hairstyles influenced the design of these millinery creations to either cover or complement one's tresses. Men's hats were more functional and all about status or part of a work uniform. However, there was a wide variety of curious-looking toppers for young men. Companies manufactured hats and individual milliners custom-made them for clients. For both men and women, there were straw hats for summer and felts hats for winter.

Headwear matched outfits and activities. You would don a riding hat to ride horses, a tall top hat in the evening, or a fancy fascinator for everyday wear. Regional variations ranged from wide-brimmed plantation straw hats for men and women to hardy felt hats for cowboys. Frontier women wore practical cotton bonnets to shield their faces and necks from the sun.

The sheer number of stylistic variations that appeared each year and decade makes it difficult to specifically name every type of hat depicted in these photographs. Occasionally, there is a match in advertisements or trade magazines. One thing is certain; no comprehensive guide to all the headgear worn by men and women in the nineteenth century exists. To research this topic, you can review fragments from examples in museums and historical societies, or those printed in photos or old catalogs and magazines. In the mid-1850s, over 7.5 million hats were sold in New York each year.[2]

When you look at the photographs of the men and women depicted in this volume or your own family photos, it's easy to jump to the conclusion that our ancestors dressed in drab colors. Nothing could be farther from the reality.

Newspaper stories describe the shapes and wide range of hat colors while hand-colored engravings in fashion magazines such as *Godey's Lady's Book*, *Petersen's Magazine,* and *Demorest's*, illustrate the colors available. For instance, during the course of my research for *Finding the Civil War in Your Family Album*, I saw a newspaper article that advised women on how to dress for pictures.

> ***How to Dress for a Photograph***
>
> *Let me offer a few words of advice touching dress. Orange color for certain optical reasons is photographically, black; blue*

is white; other shades or tone of color are proportionally darker or lighter [sic] as they contain more or less of these colors. The progressive scale of photographic color commences with the highest. The others stand thus: white, light, blue, violet, pink, mauve, dark blue, lemon, blue-green, leather brown, drab, cerise, Magenta, yellow green, dark brown, purple, red, amber, moroon [sic], orange, dead black. Complexion has to be much considered in connection with dress. Blondes can wear much lighter colors than brunettes. The latter always present better pictures in dark dresses, but neither look well in positive white. Violent contrasts of color should be especially guarded against.[3]

Newspaper articles advised women to wear colors that flattered their complexion and attire.[4] As you gaze at these images, try to imagine these hats and bonnets in subtle gray to brilliant yellow or red.

So what is the difference between a hat and a bonnet? A quick check of the *Oxford English Dictionary* turned up some curious references to that terminology. *Spoons Encyclopedia of the Industrial Arts* (1879) defined a hat as a headdress with a brim. English writer, Richard Grant White, author of *England Without and Within,* wrote "A bonnet has strings and a hat has not."[5] The interesting expression, "his hat covers his family," is a remark used to describe a person without relatives.

Fun Facts about Hats

The first baseball cap debuted in 1849.[6]

In the early nineteenth century, the popularity of the beaver hat contributed to the near extinction of the animal.

Like many men of his generation, Abraham Lincoln used to carry papers in his stovepipe hat.

In the late 1860s, a New York hat maker requested a bridge be built over Broadway to increase his business.

In the nineteenth century, political parades included men wearing torchlight hats complete with an oil lantern affixed to the front.

Real stuffed birds decorated women's hats.

In 1883, a felt hat cost $1.75 and velvet ones could be purchased for $5.00.

Factories in Danbury, Connecticut, also known as "Hat City," manufactured 6 million hats in 1890.

In 1895, New York legislators introduced a bill to require women go hatless in the theatre.

In 1897, American women spent $100 million on Easter hats, an average of $3.33 for each woman in the country.[7]

According to Jessica Ortner in Practical Millinery (1897), millinery is a collective term embracing all varieties of female headgear and has its origin in the word "Milaner, a phrase that referred to individuals from Milan.[8]"

1840-1850

A wide variety of bonnets adorned the heads of women in the 1840s and 1850s with materials adjusted according to the season. In the summer months, different types of straw—leghorn (bleached straw of Italian origin), wheat, or rice—were braided and plaited for men's hats and women's bonnets. In the winter, women's bonnets were made of velvet, satin, or silk. Married women wore lace caps, known as **day caps**,† inside, but always wore a more substantial bonnet covering when they went outdoors. There were wide-brimmed country hats for casual attire and floral wreaths and caps for evening wear.

> **Bonnet.** Iron-grey satin and terry velvet, lined with pink satin, with tuffs of terry velvet inside.[14]
> —*Boston Evening Transcript,* December 28 1847

One popular style known as the **poke bonnet** resembled a coal scuttle in shape. The poke bonnet was fitted at the back of the head and wide at the front, extending a bit past the face. The style allowed women to show off their sausage curls and left space to trim the interior of the bonnet. A piece of fabric called a curtain covered the neck in the back. Women could purchase ready-made and trimmed bonnets or buy a shell and decorate a hat to suit themselves. Trims included artificial fruits, leaves and flowers, and, birds and feathers. One very fashionable feather, the fluffy Marabou, came from the underside of the marabou

---

† Definitions of words in boldface can be found in the glossary.

Journal des Demoiselles, 1840s.

stork. These feathers could be dyed in various colors. If an authentic Marabou wasn't available, turkey feathers could be substituted. Ostrich feathers were also commonly used to adorn hats.

The owners of local shops such as Hazelton's Bonnet Saloon in Concord, New Hampshire bragged in their advertising that they bought current fashions and trims in New York and Boston. Their business also included the repair of straw bonnets, assuring customers that "all spots, perspiration removed without extra charge."[9] If you didn't live near the shop you could send them your bonnet. This shop also sold supplies such as straw or silk bonnet patterns to local milliners and merchants. No credit was accepted for these services. James Hazelton only took cash.

In Brattleboro, Vermont ladies shopped "at the sign of the big bonnet" (a wooden sign). O. Rhodes opened a store in 1848 and sold a wide variety of bonnets under various styles—"Florence, Pedal, Rutland, Bird's Eye, Coburg, Pearl, Rough and Ready, French Lace and Fancy Straw." Rhodes also carried mourning bonnets.[10] Other shops proclaimed that they carried specific styles such as a Dunstable. These names are generally derived from the place where the style was originally developed or from which the materials originated.

Mrs. Milson of New London, Connecticut, offered her customers a 25 percent discount if they shopped in her Bradley St. Bonnet Store to try to double her business. She bragged her prices were lower than what was charged in Boston and New York. She carried bonnets and leghorn hats, bleached and pressed with the French and English finish, and sold them for $.25 to $1.00.[11] French and English fashions were copied in the United States and had a certain cache.

In the 1840s, straw hat manufacturers used several types of green-cut grass such as wheat and rye. After harvesting, the stalks were bleached through scalding, exposure to the sun, and chemical treatment. While some local grass was used to produce braids or plaits of straw, a great many braids were imported from England and Italy.

According to an article in the *Boston Evening Transcript*, over 12,000 women worked in the industry. Foxborough, Massachusetts, with fewer than two thousand inhabitants, supported a manufactory that employed more than 1,300 women and close to 80 men who produced 266,260 bonnets worth $320,000 dollars.[12]

In this period, many men wore stovepipe hats with narrow brims and tall crowns. Earlier in the century, beaver fur was the material of choice for these hats, but overhunting of the animal depleted the population. Beaver hats had a particular advantage. They were waterproof. By the 1840s, manufacturers processed felted silk to resemble beaver when making men's tall hats. There were various shaped hats for men with small crowns and curled brims as well as wide-brimmed straw boaters. Small-crowned hats with broad brims made from beaver were commonly known as "**wide-awakes**."

Definition of a Bonnet

The following definition of a bonnet by a wag, is very good... for the back part of a lady's head–designed to keep her hair up and to show ... outlines of a beautiful forehead.[13]

—*Ohio Statesman, March 1, 1842*

A Seedy Bonnet A bonnet was exhibited at the Institute in Niblo's Garden, New York, made of melon seed. It contained 8,763 seeds and 17,776 stitches, each taken with a needle! A very curious bonnet, no doubt, but rather a seedy affair, according to our notion.[15]

—*Times-Picayune.* October 30, 1840

Philander Chase (1775-1852) Bishop of Protestant Episcopal Church. Mathew Brady, photographer.

He wears a soft wool clerical cap. Chase held office between 1843-1852.

Dolley Madison (1768-1849).

Former First Lady Dolley Madison wears her signature **turban**, fashionable during the War of 1812. Older or conservative women often wore older style hats. This picture was taken in approximately 1848.

Godey's Lady's Book, **February, 1841.**

This Godey's fashion plate shows how far forward women's bonnets extended and framed the front of the face.

Godey's Lady's Book, **December, 1849.**

Godey's Lady's Book featured instructions for how to make this opera cap from white and rose-colored German wool, steel meshes, and white chenille.

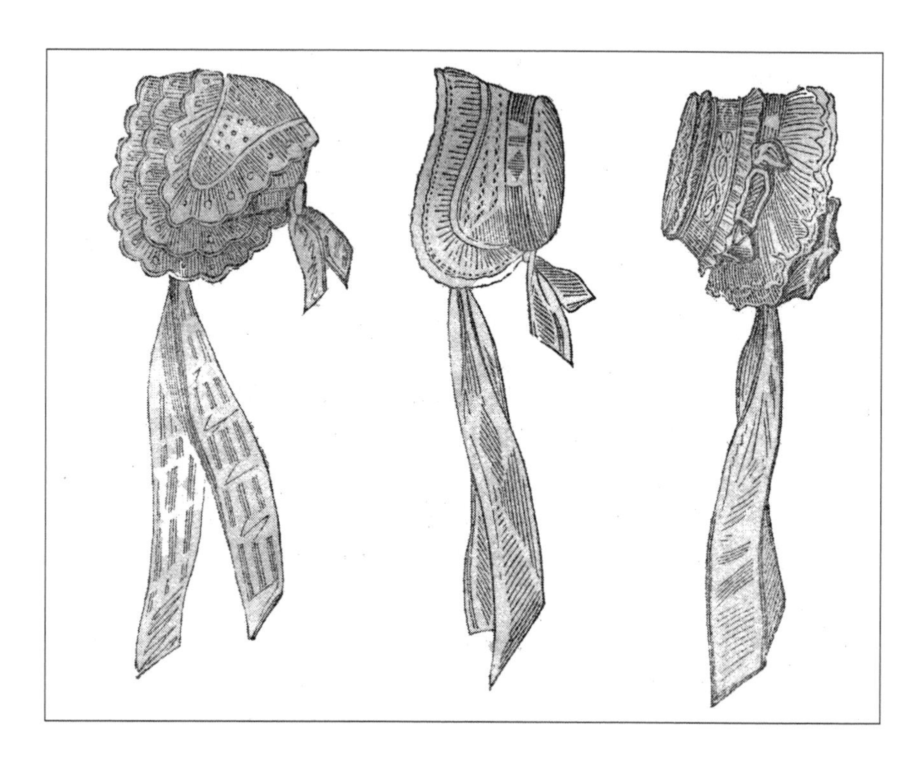

Different style bonnets were worn for day and evening or for outdoors and indoors. Married women wore day caps over their hair. These were to be made from India muslin.

> *Advice from Godey's:*
>
> *No unmarried lady should wear a morning cap; it is the mark, the badge, if we may so call it, of the young matron. And if the wife cares as much for her husband's admiration after marriage as before it, she will never dispense with this tasteful coquettish appendage to a morning toilette.*[16]
>
> —*Godey's Lady's Book, December 1849.*

Daguerreotype of an unidentified woman, 1840s.

This woman wears a day cap with a frilled edge. Her dress has a lovely lace collar.

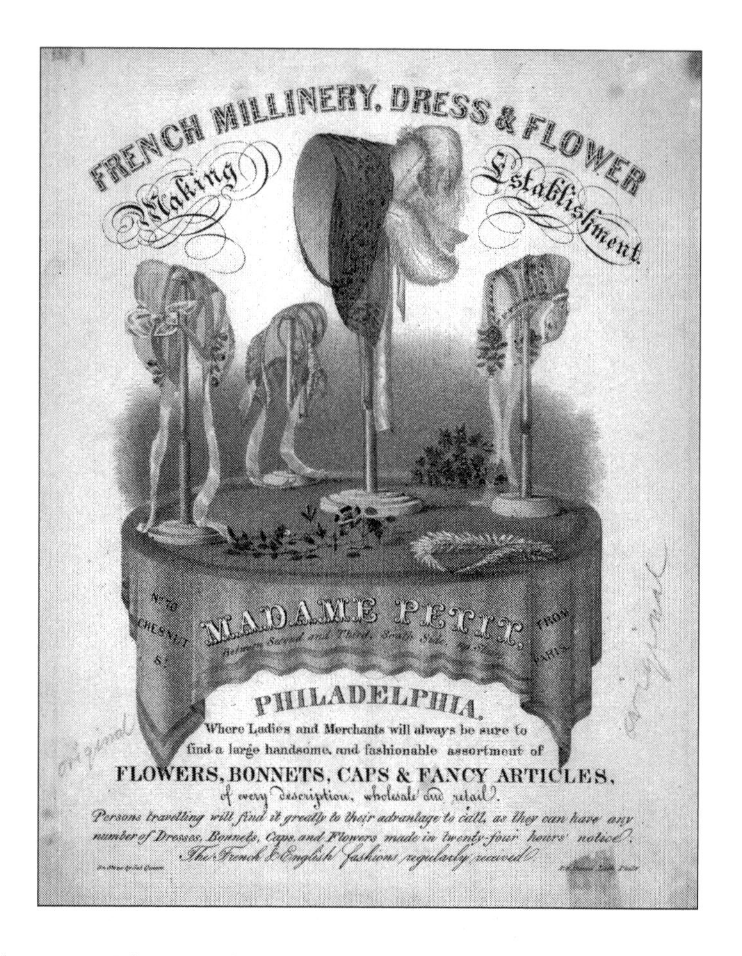

Madame Petit's French Millinery, Dress & Flower Making Establishment.

According to the advertisement depicted in the image above, Madame Petit sold her wares directly to customers as well as to resellers. A client could buy dresses, caps, and flowers. On display in this ad is an assortment of day caps and a bonnet embellished with flowers. French styles were considered quite fashionable and were sought after by American women. Contemporary fashion magazines such as *Godey's Lady's Book* often published fashion plates of "Americanized French Fashions."

Unidentified couple, 1840s, Warren, Cambridgeport, MA.

In this late 1860s or early 1870s copy of an 1840s daguerreotype, this elderly couple wears simple clothing. On the woman's head is a day cap with side ruffles. A fan-pleated bodice adds style to her cotton dress while her companion wears a double-breasted coat with large buttons. The woman also wears glasses.

Unidentified men, late 1840s or early 1850s.

According to the Library of Congress cataloging record, this is an occupational portrait. These men "hold floor rammer and foundry tools used for packing sand against molds." Their soft hats feature high crowns and short flat brims. The man on the left wears his hat at a rakish angle.

1850-1860

In the 1850s, bonnets no longer shielded the wearer's face. Bonnets sat halfway back on the head and framed the face. In the early years of the decade, the front edge flared out. Both hairstyles and decorative trims, like those of the 1840s, were visible—flowers, ribbons, and, in this decade, even feathers. Simpler bonnets had tulle ruching on the inside framing the face. Just like today, it was younger women who maintained the fashion, while their older contemporaries resisted the new styles.

In the mid-1850s, the following description of a bonnet appeared in the *Weekly Wisconsin Patriot*, "The fashionable bonnet is well described as falling off the head, reclining languishingly on the shoulders as though it were too weak, poor think to hold itself up, and was going off in a kind of fashionable swoon."[17] Fashion icon Empress Eugenie's attire was followed in the newspaper. It was reported that "altho' the bonnet of the Empress Eugenie displays fully, her face and hair, it does not convey to the beholder the idea of its being likely to fall from the head behind, but rather seems to cling to and support the hair in that position."[18] Veils were usually worn thrown back but sometimes in front of the face.

The invention of artificial dyes in the 1850s led to the introduction of new colors. William Perkin accidently discovered that coal tar produced a bright purple color which he called mauvine. The artificial dyes didn't fade over time like natural dyes did. Perkin continued his experiments to develop Britannia Violet and Perkin's Green. Throughout the decade, chemists produced new colors—magenta,

Martius yellow, bleu de Lyon and aldehyde green. These bright colors became quite popular in the 1860s.

Headdresses replaced day caps with symmetrical arrangements of flowers, lace, and feathers. Women no longer hid their hair while indoors. Instead, they decorated it. An illustration in *Frank Leslie's Gazette* for August 1858 shows small caps trimmed and decorated with artificial flowers, lace, and velvet with long ribbons trailing down the neck.

Summer was for straw hats. Making these hats was a multi-step process that involved harvesting the straw, drying it in the sun, dipping it into glue, and then shaping the hat using specially made plaster blocks. When dry, the semi-formed hat was placed on a special wooden block. In a separate room, operators used a machine operated with a foot lever to press the hats. During the pressing process, the hats were heated but covered with a cloth to prevent scorching. In the Union Straw Works, based in Foxborough, Massachusetts, the next stop was workers' apartments where young girls sewed cloth-covered wire around the edges or the inside paper lining. After this, the hats went to the shaping room where they were placed again on blocks for shaping and finishing. Other employees added trim.[19] Braiding the straw was primarily women's work.

One woman rose to fame in Massachusetts and across the country as a result of her hats. In the late eighteenth century, Betsy Baker of Norfolk County, Massachusetts copied a bonnet she saw in a store and created a straw hat industry. The *Lowell Daily Citizen and News* reported that Baker's Massachusetts-based business employed 10,000 people and manufactured six thousand bonnets and hats each year.[20]

In 1856, an English doctor said in the *Sun* that the new bonnets caused health issues in his female patients. "I have to lament the great increase amongst the female part of my practice, of the doloreux in the forehead, loss of sight and great suffering in the ear, induced, I firmly believe, from the present absurd fashion of dressing the neck instead of the head."[21] He advocated for a change in fashion.

The styles of bonnets waxed and waned from year to year as did the decorative elements. In the fall of 1857, trimmings were

C. Henry Richardson as a blocker, 1858, Medway, MA.
The hat block was used to shape headgear. The town of Medway, Massachusetts had a straw hat factory.

primarily made from feathers of the same color as the bonnet. Lace trims were also common. "The lace called "l'Imperatrice," resembling the trimming for mantillas, which originated in the last season. It was generally brown, blue or green, but in different shades."[22] Bonnets made of this lace were decorated with ostrich or Maribou feathers of the same color of the bonnet. From the mid-1850s to the mid-1860s, one of the most popular hat styles for women was known as a **porkpie**, so named because it resembled a pie with a flat crown and a rolled brim that often had long trailing ribbons. There was a similarly shaped hat for men.

Men in the 1850s saw a change in the style of their headgear. Tall stovepipe hats were advocated as being healthier in warm weather. The shape and height of the stovepipe crown allowed extra air circulation versus the small round crowned hats that fit close to the head.

At the London World's Fair of 1851, stovepipe hats, with straight sides made from beaver or other fur, were starting to be replaced by soft, round crowned felt.[23] Hats often reflected a man's economic status or his political leanings. Merchants Salaman & Booth of Milwaukee introduced "Fremont Hats" which they expected to sell quickly.[24] In 1852, better quality men's hats sold for about $3 or $4.

The Love Knot (first stanza)
by Nora Perry

Tying her bonnet under her chin,
She tied her raven ringlets in.
But not alone in the silken snare
Did she catch her lovely floating hair,
For, tying her bonnet under her chin,
She tied a young man's heart within[25]

—*New York Herald-Tribune,*
January 12, 1858.

How to Make a Fashionable Bonnet

Take a diamond-shaped piece of lace or muslin; slightly round the obtuse angles; stiffen the edges with wire, and put strings on the ends, to fasten it under the chin. Trim it all around the edges with a profusion of lace, flowers and bows, making very little distinction between the front and the back. Tie it over the back of the head, or let it hang between the shoulders, taking good care not to let it come forward so as to cover the top of the head, much less shade the face. If of very light thin materials, it may be worn indifferently as a cap or bonnet. N.B. Be sure to fasten on the strings strongly, for if lost its loss would hardly be felt or discovered.[26]

—*Barre Patriot,* August 4, 1854.

New Styles of Bonnet

A new style of bonnet has lately appeared. It is formed of taffetas, the front of which is indented at equal distances, and trimmed with double ruches of narrow blond, the curtain being trimmed in the same manner. Upon one side of the front is a rose, composed of velvet blond and feathers, accompanied with leaves of crape, worked with velvet inside; the front trimmed with the same flower, of a smaller size, mixed with rosebuds placed high up and ruches of tulle below. The ruches are sometimes replaced by blonde and very small flowers.[27]

—*St. Paul Daily Pioneer,* February 13, 1855.

Summer Bonnets

The fashion columns of the metropolitan journals have the following in regard to the summer bonnet question. It will interest our lady reader, no doubt: The favorite materials at present for dress bonnets are sea green and lilac crape, over a thin lace foundation with small white flowers and violets in clusters and wreaths. Chip and fine straw are much in vogue, and the trimming preferred to ribbon is made of knots of chip or straw bows mingled with pale-hued or unobtrusive flowers. Straws often have a similar wreath laid over the top of the bonnet, in the centre of a circle bordered by black lace. Ladies who wish to travel, or spend much time in the country, provide themselves with shirred bonnets, composed of brown pine-apple fabric. This material will take the place of the lawn bonnet during the coming season; and is equally serviceable in resisting the dust and dampness, while it has a much more dressy appearance. In black it makes a pretty mourning bonnet.[28]

—*Plain Dealer,* May 26, 1859.

Unidentified daguerreotype, 1850s.

In the 1850s, bonnets were worn back on the head and tied in place with wide ribbons. Notice the white ruffled trim on the inside edge of this woman's bonnet. It appears to be a drawn silk bonnet of the mid-1850s. Her scalloped-edged lace collar further accessorizes her outfit. A cape and a pair of gloves complete the look.

Unidentified daguerreotype, 1850s.

Big silk ties held bonnets in place. They were not only functional. The tied bow served as a fashion statement. This woman's bonnet has minimal trim. Instead, she relies on her symmetrically braided hair to frame her face.

Unidentified daguerreotype, 1855-57.

This woman decorated the inside of her winter bonnet with rosettes and ruffled net. Her tie is likely a light color that matched the flowers. The dark fabric hanging down from the sides of the bonnet is known as a curtain. It covered the neck. She wears a lovely cape. Her white lace undersleeves and fingerless mitts are visible at the bottom of the image.

Unidentified daguerreotype, 1850s.

This woman's muslin day cap has a ruffle at the side of her head and is neatly tied under her chin. In the 1850s, women wore wide lace collars. The collar on this dress is scalloped.

Unidentified elderly couple, 1850s.

The woman in this photo wears a cap featuring long ribbons and flowers. While she's elderly, she doesn't have a white hair on her head. Her companion, however, has a full head of white hair. This could be due to the use of hair dye or because photographic methods only picked up certain colors, turning the rest dark. Instead of the traditional white lace, this woman's collar appears to be a dark color, or is perhaps even black.

Unidentified man, 1850s.

A wide-brimmed straw hat was a fashion requirement for men in the warm summer months. The hat in this photo has a slight curled brim and features a dark ribbon band around the crown. This man, who stares directly into the camera, is nicely framed by the scalloped-edge photographic mat, one of the many styles available in the 1850s.

Unidentified man, 1850s.

Another man with a direct gaze wears a felt porkpie hat in this image. The decorative mat on this image nicely emphasizes the velvet collar and wide lapels on the man's jacket.

Unidentified woman, between 1851 and 1860, Mathew Brady, photographer.

A frothy looking cap sits on the back of this woman's head. She has her hair clasped at the sides. This portrait captures a thoughtful expression. Ordinary folks, wealthy individuals, and the famous visited photographer Mathew Brady's studios in New York and Washington.

Elizabeth Cady Stanton (1815-1902) and her daughter Harriot (1856-1940). 1856. Photograph of a daguerreotype.

In this image, Stanton wears the popular style bonnet that was worn back on the head. Tucked into the brim are flowers. Stanton was a well-known abolitionist and women's rights advocate. She presented the Declaration of Sentiments at Seneca Falls, New York, at a women's rights convention. The document, based on the United States Declaration of Independence, stated that men and women were created equal.

Louisa Van Velsor Whitman (1795-1873), 1851-1860.

In the 1850s, Louisa Whitman, the mother of American literary genius Walt Whitman, wears a fashionable cap with long ties. As was common in the 1850s, she keeps the ties unfastened. In this portrait, Whitman smiles for the camera. She wears a patterned cotton dress.

William Bradhurst, 1851-1860.

In this daguerreotype taken by Rufus Anson, Bradhurst wears a popular felted hat with a short crown, flat top, and an upturned brim. According to the Library of Congress cataloging record, Bradhurst's father was Samuel Bradhurst. His light-colored eyes are barely visible in this picture.

William Sidney Mount (1807-1868). Daguerreotype date probably between 1853-1860.

Mathew Brady's studio took this daguerreotype of the very well-dressed genre painter Mount, depicted here with a full beard. He wears a tall-crowned top hat likely made from silk. He's posed in a slight profile with his coat draped over his arm. At his feet, you can see the wooden foot of the brace that holds him still for the picture.

Gertrude Mercer McCurdy Hubbard (1827-1909).

Taken between 1855 and 1859, this young mother wears a hat with tulle ruching on the inside and a lace veil pulled back for the photograph. Her bonnet has a lace veil, which Hubbard has pulled back for the portrait of herself and her young infant. Hubbard was the great grandmother of inventor Alexander Graham Bell.

Unidentified woman, 1850s.

A slightly ruffled muslin cap sits atop this woman's simple curled hairstyle. Her dress features a small lace collar accented by a brooch. A paisley shawl adds detail to this classic portrait.

Unidentified woman, 1850s.

This well-dressed woman wears a day cap with ruffles on the sides and long lace ties. A thin ribbon appears to be tied under the chin. Her silk dress has a wide lace collar. Her white muslin undersleeves peek out from her sleeves. She wears fingerless gloves called mitts. Beside her, paisley fabric covers the table.

Unidentified woman, 1850s.

This woman wears the long ends of the cap tied under her chin. With its ruffled sides, the cap sits back on her head. In an interested pose, the woman gazes at the camera in a sidelong glance. The mat for this daguerreotype is decorated with a botanical motif.

Unidentified elderly woman, 1850s.

This older woman wears a dark-colored cap. The August 1858 issue of *Frank Leslie's Gazette* showed variations of these caps made with bows, velvet, tulle, and flowers. In this case, the lace cap is adorned with plaid ribbon, visible in this side view. The woman's silk dress has lace at the elbow, white undersleeves, and a white collar.

Horace Greeley (1811-1872), Mathew Brady, photographer.

Hats for men often offered clues into their station in life, their aspirations, or their occupation. Newspaper man Horace Greeley was a fashion icon of his time, ridiculed for his choice of chin hair. He posed for this portrait with a folded newspaper in his lap and dressed for outdoors in his heavy overcoat. His hat is tipped back on his head.

1860-1870

Throughout the 1860s, bonnets were still small and worn at the back of the head. Faces continued to be framed rather than shielded by the bonnet. High-crowned spoon bonnets (so called because of the high brim), heart-shaped bonnets, and soft brimmed Fanchon-style bonnets were all popular. Small hats for women began to replace bonnets and were similar to versions worn by their fathers and brothers. At home, women wore day caps, muslin caps meant for indoor use and to be worn under bonnets.

While some men still wore top hats, such as stovepipe hats like those favored by President Abraham Lincoln, a wide variety of smaller hats (brimmed and brimless), **bowlers**, derby style, and caps were available. Styles ranged from Eton caps and felt bowlers to small straw hats for the summer months. These came with a ribbon known as Nattie's. Hats worn by workers differed from those worn by gentlemen. Work hats were made of soft felt or resembled caps with a small brim in the front. The tall stovepipe hats like those sported by Lincoln were also functional—the President often carried important papers in that tall hat.

In the late 1860s, hat maker John Genin advocated to the New York City Common Council that placing a bridge across busy Broadway at Fulton Street would increase the number of customers who visited his store. The bridge was built enabling pedestrians to safely cross the road and not risk death from horse-drawn vehicles. Two year later, rival hat makers, Charles Knox and his allies, sued New York City for the removal of the Loew Bridge. Knox alleged the bridge adversely affected his business by causing his storefront to be in shadow. He won and the bridge, built in 1866, was torn down in 1868.

Men were not without their own style icons. In 1860, it was the Prince of Wales. According to the *San Francisco Bulletin*, "The Prince's visit has done something to encourage this imitation of the Anglican modes, even to the extent of copying the abominable hats, which everybody in the Royal party wore, from the Prince downward. Such a collection of shocking bad hats was never seen except on scarecrows in a corn field. They all had wide brims, or else turned up awkwardly at the edges and had a full luster, as if they had been extensively rained upon."[29]

A visit from the Prince of Wales in 1860 influenced men's fashions. Here, the Prince of Wales poses with his brother Prince Alfred. Window & Bridge, London.

The wide variety of military headgear worn during the Civil War was based on the unit or branch in which a man served and on one's status as an officer or enlisted man. Puffed Whipple caps, slouch hats, broad-brimmed low-crowned felt hats, standard issue forage caps, Hardee hats, and a style known as the McDowell cap that had a bump in the back were all common. You can see examples of these cap styles in *A Guide to U.S. Army Dress Helmets, 1872-1904.*

During the Civil War, soldiers wore long-crowned kepis or hats that were wider at the bottom and featured branch insignia letters on the front. Cavalry regiments wore wide- brimmed tall-crowned Hardee hats, designed by William Hardee, a Lieutenant General in the Confederate Army and a West Point graduate. The brim of this hat was generally pinned up on the right side for cavalry and artillery and on the left for infantry. A feather and a wool cord decorated these hats.

Secession Bonnet

The *Charleston Mercury* gives the following description of a bonnet worn by a Southern Carolina lady: "The bonnet is composed of white and black Georgia Cotton, covered with a network of black cotton, the streamers ornamented with palmetto trees and a lone star, embroidered with gold thread, while the feathers are formed of white and black worsted." Can't some of our Connecticut girls rig up a bonnet distinctive of that much-abused State? Trim it with pumpkin vines, squash-buds and cherry-ripes, and adorn it with cord tassels and wooden nutmegs.[30]

—*Philadelphia Inquirer,* December 25, 1860.

About Bonnets

A black bonnet with white feathers, with white rose, or red flowers, suit a fair complexion. A lustreless white bonnet does not suit well with fair and rosy complexions. It is otherwise with bonnets of gause, crape or lace. They are suitable to all complexions.[31]

—Macon Telegraph, June 11, 1865.

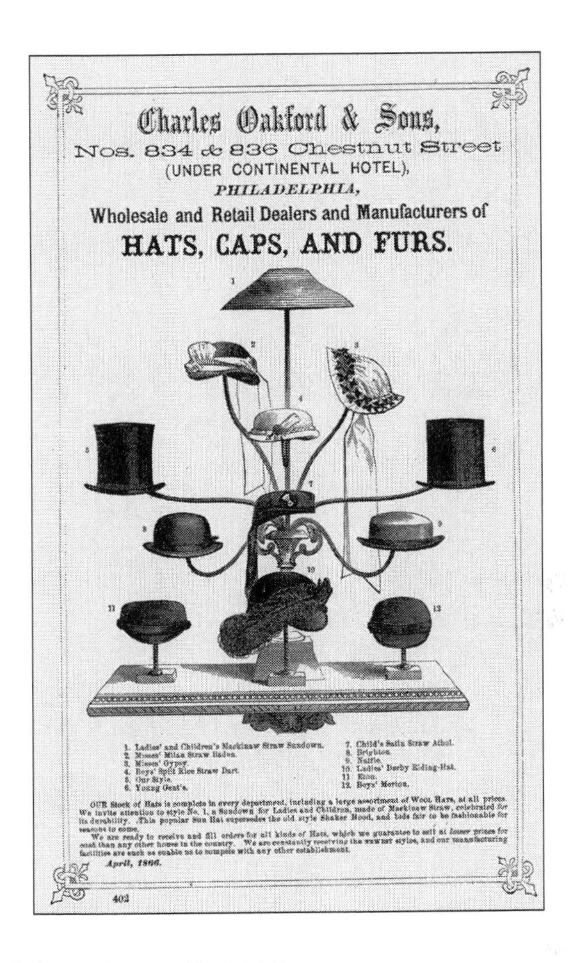

Godeys' Lady's Book, April, 1866.

This display ad shows off twelve different styles of hats for all ages. At the top is a Mackinaw Straw Sundown hat. Below that, the three styles (left to right) are —a Milan Straw Baden, a boy's spilt Rice Straw Dart, and a Gypsy. On the next level, two top hats appear. The one shown on the left was designed by the store while the hat on the right, with the flatter brim, was meant for young men. On the second row from the bottom, the hat on the left is a Brighton, a child's Satin Straw Athol holds the center position, and the very popular style known as the Nattie appears to the right. A woman's riding hat in the derby style takes the center position in the bottom and is flanked by two hats for boys—an Eton on the left and a Morton on the right.

Unidentified group, 1860s.

Top hats came in all different sizes. In this case, the man on the left wears an extremely tall hat in a light-colored fabric while the man to the right wears a small hat with an upturned brim. It's likely that both women owned bonnets, but didn't wear them for this photo.

Unidentified couple, late 1860s.

The woman's small hat is decorated with a veil and flowers. Her companion wears a broad-brimmed hat with a band around the crown and contrast trim at the edge of the brim. This photo is unusual because it's rare to see women holding purses. You can also see the edge of her hoop near the bottom of her skirt.

An unidentified group portrait. Bundy & Williams, 314 & 326 Chapel St., New Haven, CT.

The women carry patterned shawls and wear small bonnets that cover just the crown of the head in the style of the 1860s. The woman on the far left wears a fanchon bonnet with the heart-shaped center. Bonnets featured wide silk ties worn in a large bow under the chin.

Unidentified man in a leather cap, circa late 1860s.

The subject dressed in a collared shirt, vest, and suit for this photo. His cap is an unusual style.

Unidentified tintype, 1860s.

This man's soft felt hat was made for everyday wear. His gingham work shirt has a band collar. Basic casual attire for men in this era consisted of a shirt, vest, and jacket.

Godey's Lady's Book, October, 1864.

Left to right:

A white silk bonnet, with a double cape of Eugenie blue silk. The bonnet is bound with blue silk, and the puffing is made of the same material. Black and white grasses with a few scarlet berries are arranged on the outside of the bonnet, and also form part of the inside trimming.

A white silk drawn bonnet, edged with black velvet and white drop buttons. The trimming is composed of crimson tulips and white feathers.

A black Neapolitan bonnet, with a white crepe cape covered with white blonde (a type of fabric). The trimming of the bonnet is black lace, black ribbon, and salmon-colored flowers.

Unidentified woman, 1860s.

This woman wears a bonnet with an oversized bow. This is a winter outfit. A heavy cape covers her dress.

Unidentified tintype of a woman, 1860s.

The subject wears a patterned dress of cotton fabric and a high-brimmed spoon bonnet. In the 1860s, photographic mats often had decorative elements to make them look like wooden frames. Note the printed frame that surrounds the image and the tassels.

Unidentified man, 1860s.

This man poses for the camera with a gun tucked into his waistband and an oversize brimmed top hat rakishly placed on his head. He appears to be clowning for this portrait. He sits on an overturned box.

Unidentified tintype, late 1860s.

While bonnets were the standard attire for fashionable women in the 1840s and 1850s, a new type of headgear appeared in the late 1860s—the hat modeled after those worn by men. The deep brim on this felt hat has a large feather for accent.

Possibly Emma Cochran, 1860s.

This woman wears clothing meant for horseback riding. She is holding a riding crop. Riding attire typically included fitted jackets, long sleeves, and small hats.

Unidentified woman, 1860s, Prescott & Gage, Hartford, CT.

This hat with a gathered crown and a deep folded brim is called a toque and is accented with a braided greenery.

Grandma Austin nee Houston, circa 1870.

In the 1860s, bonnets were worn far back of the head with slight decorative elements at the top of the head. Here, it's flowers. This hat is fastened with a wide ribbon. The woman wears an oversize necklace with a leather belt at her waist. She's taken off one glove for her portrait.

Possibly a member of the Hahn or Hoppe Family, circa 1869.

Small flat straw hats topped with flowers and a ribbon were popular in this era. The woman's outfit is a perfect summer combination of flowered hat and cotton dress. A photograph album sits on top of the paisley cloth on the table.

Unidentified woman in winter wear, late 1860s/early 1870s.

Bonnets were worn back on the head, while hats were worn low over the forehead, like this elliptical style hat with gathered brim and dotted netting, meant to cover the face. This style was known as a "fancy hat."

Unidentified young woman, late 1860s.

Summer heat called for straw sun hats with wide brims. They were cool and protected the head and face from the sun. A wide ribbon has been wrapped around the crown of this woman's hat. She's also draped her shoulders with a windowpane shawl. Her hair is in a net which is tied in a bow at the top of her head.

Unidentified young man, 1860s.

Graduation caps are nothing new. This happy young man poses with a toothy grin. He wears a mortarboard graduation cap with a tassle, just like today's graduates. He wears military trousers and is likely a cadet. The handcolored tassle, bow tie, and gold chain add life to this image.

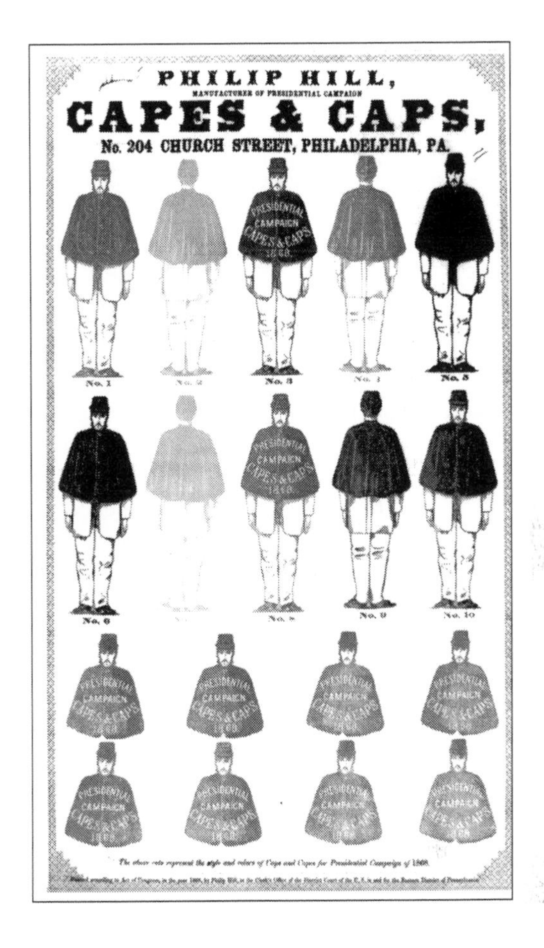

Advertisement for Philip Hill, manufacturer of capes and caps for the presidential campaign of 1868 of Horatio Seymour versus Ulysses S. Grant. Library of Congress.

Men purchased hats and capes to wear in political torchlight parades to show their support for a particular candidate. By the late nineteenth century, these parades could last for several hours. In this advertisement, you can see the emblazoned capes worn in 1868. Hats worn in these parades featured oil and wicks in a canister affixed to the front of the headgear.[32]

Unidentified man, Burrows and Bundy, 1860s, Middletown, CT.

Men's hats came in a variety of shapes and styles from small school-boy caps to wide-brimmed hats to tall stovepipe hats. This man is holding a summer straw hat with a narrow band and piping around the brim. The most prominent feature of this portrait is his hat.

Unidentified woman, 1860s.

In the 1860s, women gathered their hair into nets. This side view of a **snood**, a decorative hairnet, shows a bow on the top of the woman's head.

Unidentified mother and child, late 1860s.

This simple everyday straw hat was decorated with flowers around the brim. The mother's hat is very similar to those shown in the June 1867 edition of *Godey's Lady's Book.* The baby wears the latest style of clothing trimmed with braid and a ruffled toque.

Hoods were stylish in the 1850s and 1860s. They were meant to be worn to special events such as the opera and parties.

> *Made of white cashmere, braided with black velvet, and trimmed with cherry-colored ribbon. The tassel is of black lace.*[33]
>
> —*Godey's Lady's Book, January 1863.*

Unidentified Quaker woman, 1860s.

Quaker attire was simple. This woman wears a muslin day cap. On her lap is her bonnet with a pleated back and long front that shielded the face. A simple shawl covers her shoulders.

Private Albert H. Davis of Company K, 6th New Hampshire Infantry Regiment in uniform and Hardee Hat, mid 1860s.

He's carrying a Model 1841 Mississippi rifle, a sword and a bayonet as well as a bedroll, canteen and haversack. A haversack is similar to a backpack but it has a single strap.

Cavalry regiments wore wide brimmed tall crowned Hardee hats, designed by William Hardee, who was a Lieutenant General in the Confederate Army and a West Point graduate. The brim of this hat was generally pinned up on the right side for cavalry and artillery and on the left for infantry. A feather and wool cord decorated these hats.

Unidentified soldier, mid 1860s.

He wears the uniform of the 56th New York Volunteers (10th Legion) and a style of headgear known as a forage cap. There were many different styles of uniform caps depending on the unit. For example, the Zouave units sported small fez caps and Turkish-style pants.

Unidentified woman, 1860s, Frank Hays, London, England.

A small bonnet sits on the back of her head while beautiful trimmed netting drapes off the back. A large bow ties under her chin.

Unidentified man, early 1860s. Johnson, Scranton, PA.

In this carte de visite, the man wears his hat at a rakish angle. A man could use his hat to express personality, status, and even politics.

Unidentified man, 1860s.

This man's flat brimmed straw hat tells us that the picture was taken in the summer months, when such hats were popular. Throughout the latter half of the nineteenth century, straw hats came in a variety of shapes with various trims and ribbons. This hat has a shallow crown and a wide ribbon with a bow at the side. The photographer has posed him to show off the side view of the hat.

Unidentified group of men, circa 1870.

Two young men in shiny new top hats pose with a friend in a round tilted hat.

Unidentified man, 1860s.

This man means business. He has a direct gaze, stylish clothes, (complete with a polka dot vest), and a serious looking sturdy hat with a curved brim and a buckled band.

Unidentified young man, late 1860s.

A tall lad stands next to a photographic posing chair. On his head is a soft cap usually worn by young men or those who were off to work for the day. There is a hole in this tintype.

1870-1880

Women's hairstyles—large buns and enormous braids worn on the top of the head—influenced the shape, style, and size of hats in this decade. Small hats and bonnets dominated. Tiny tipped hats seem dwarfed by the popular dress bustles. Women added floral arrangements, feathers, ribbons, and velvet trim to their hats, perhaps in an attempt to balance the look of their ensemble.

In the beginning of the decade, long sausage curls were accented by the trailing ribbons that appeared on the small hats worn tilted forward on the head. Hats were precariously perched on the head while bonnets sat on the back of the head tied under the chin with a wide ribbon. As the hairstyles changed, so did the hats. Wide-brimmed **Gainsborough** hats sat on top of the simpler hairstyles. There were also hair decorations such as flowers and natural looking arrangements that can be considered head wear as well as large combs stuck in back buns or decorative tiaras that were worn towards the front of the head.

Women seeking fashion advice turned to the popular women's magazines that featured colored plates and plentiful engravings such as *Godey's Lady's Book* or *Peterson's Magazine.* These publications also offered instructions on how to make simple indoor caps.

Every season, hat manufacturers and milliners developed new designs with unique names. In 1877, the high-squared crown Devonshire hat replaced the "Mother Goose" and featured a "broader crown, less conical and narrower brim.[34]

After the Centennial Exhibition of 1876, Spanish mantillas were worn as hair coverings. Around the time of the centennial, women's hats and bonnets were taller. Bonnets with upturned brims featured large looped ribbons and floral arrangements.

English walking hats with Derby crowns reappeared. Another new shape resembled a riding hat, with a high crown, and rolled back rim.

According to newspaper stories, hats were made in a wide variety of colors and shades. The range of reds included Geranium red, pink coral, red coral, and a red-brown. Yellow was the most popular color—buttercup, dandelions, jonquils, mandarin, old gold, a yellow brown, maize, corn color, straw, and tea rose. A sickly frog green was common as was salmon. Basic colors of cream, white, and gray were also available.[35]

At the turn of the decade, fancy hats made entirely from feathers appeared alongside the standard straw hats and those made from velvet or satin. For the less fashion-conscious woman, "poke" bonnets could still be purchased.[36] Hats adorned by large ostrich feathers, large bows, or brilliant groups of flowers were common.

Straw hats derived their names from the type of straw used in the manufacturing process. In other cases, the names were linked to the country where the style had originated. For instance, leghorn straw came from Italy while **Panama** hats were made from a plant found in Ecuador.

The leaf of this plant was cut off before it opened, then sliced into strips. "The split leaf, which is of a greenish white color, is next dipped into boiling water, then into tepid water acidulated with lemon juice and lastly it is allowed to soak in cold water then left to dry. Each hat is made from a single leaf. [37]

Men's hats of straw, felt, wool, or silk were available. In the colder climates, fur hats remained popular. In 1876, $3.5 million worth of men's hats were sold. Hats in all the styles from previous decades had become so affordable even laborers could purchase them.

The New Hat and the New Bonnet

When the great millinery openings for the season have taken place and the newest and prettiest styles in bonnets, hats, caps and nondescript articles in head-gear displayed, it is not to be supposed that we are to be confined to one shape or one style in hats or bonnets. So far from this the shapes are multitudious almost as the sands upon the sea-shore, and if long faces or round faces, or square faces, or faces with no shape at all, do not get the frame to suit them, it must be that they are unaware of their own peculiarities and their own requirements, and not because they can not be met.[38]

—*Galveston Weekly News,* October 15, 1877.

"Lorraine, Alsatian and Normandy Bows"

Of these bows for the coiffure the Lorraine is the newest, and a still higher bow than the Alsatian and Normandy. It is more effective from the fact that it is narrower, and there is more of the butterfly form, which the Alsatian suggests. The Lorraine is of plain ribbon, two loops of black and two of yellow, the cross piece being of both colors. It is also made of pink and black or red and black, the lower "wing" of the left side is black and the upper wing of the right, thus giving the parti-colored effect.

The Alsatian increases in breadth, brocaded ribbons being the favorites for this huge, double winged butterfly bow, as broad as it is high. The Normandy bow ought to be of black velvet, and that alone; but the caprice of fashion fancying the shape has it now in ribbon of every hue and kind. It is lower and of narrower ribbon than the Alsatian and spreads out on the sides instead of rising a foot above the brow. Some Normandy bows have long ends, which cross at the back and hang below the braided hair.[39]

—*New York Herald*, March 23, 1879.

Unidentified man, circa 1870.

The man in this tintype photo wears a porkpie hat which he has positioned at a jaunty angle. His tiny bow tie was fashionable for men in this decade. Both his jacket and his hat suggest he posed in cold weather.

Journal Des Demoiselles, 1870s.

These fashion plates depict a variety of decorated hats from France. These would be adapted for American wearers.

Unidentified women, circa 1875.

In this decade, a wide variety of hats and bonnets came into fashion. The medium-size crown on this woman's hat has been decorated with flowers. She wears the hat tilted forward, low on the forehead in the style of the 1870s. The woman on the right wears an elaborately patterned paisley shawl.

Unidentified men, 1870s.

Top hats were a standard form of head covering for men. In the 1870s, these hats were worn primarily by men in prominent positions or for special occasions. Men turned to everyday caps and hats for casual dress. In these two tintypes, the men use fringed studio chairs as a prop.

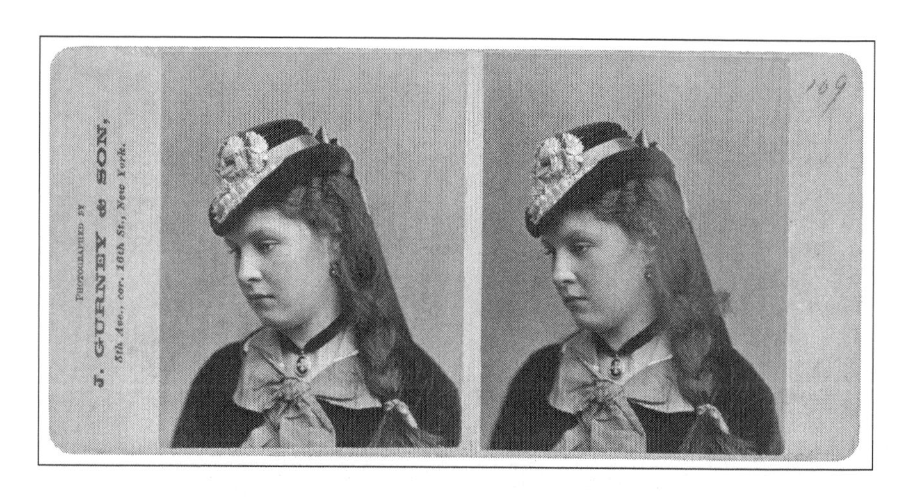

Marianne "Minnie" Conway, circa 1870. *Photographed by J. Gurney & Son, New York.*

This bright yellow stereograph depicts Marianne "Minnie" Conway. An actress, Conway took over management of the Brooklyn Theater after the death of her father in 1874. Her life became the focus of media attention after she first married a coronet player, and later, an actor. In this image, she wears her hair in a loose braid. The plush hat makes the perfect accompaniment to her silk ribbon and velvet neck ribbon with charm. These stereo cards were collected in sets.

Unidentified couple, mid-late1870s.

This woman wears a striped straw hat with a high crown and an upturned brim on one side. Her companion holds a soft felted wool hat with wide brim and band. Her sleeves feature ruffled cuffs and she wears a simple scarf around her neck. The man sports a work shirt with a loose-fitting jacket.

Unidentified young man, 1870s.

This is a very modern looking but dented soft felt hat with a narrow brim, high crown, and wide brim.

Unidentified woman, 1870s.

This late 1860s or early 1870s hat is decorated with flowers, ribbon, and greenery. A long ribbon trails down the back. The woman's hair is in a net. It was common practice in the 1870s to pose leaning on a piece of upholstered furniture with a rolled side.

Unidentified young woman, 1870s.

Instead of wearing a hat, this woman has accessorized with a flowered headpiece set on her braided hair. It's a youthful style. The neck scarf serves as a collar.

Unidentified young woman, 1870s.

This young lady stares directly into the camera. Her straw **boater** is tilted forward in the style of the 1870s. The hat appears to be made of a colored straw. The beaded collar and fringe on her jacket complete the look.

Unidentified woman, 1870s.

Smaller hats such as the one shown here accommodated the large hairstyles of the 1870s. This hat is a dramatic presentation of a large light-colored feather, a real stuffed bird, and gathered fabric. She displays a clasped group of curls over one shoulder. Her simple wool coat contrasts with her extravagant hat.

Unidentified young woman, 1869-1875.

This smartly dressed young woman wears a small bonnet adorned with spring flowers. It ties on the side so as not to compete with the bow at the neckline.

Unidentified woman, after 1876.

After the Centennial Exposition of 1876, Spanish mantillas like this were considered quite stylish.

Unidentified woman, circa 1876, A.M. Zumbro's Art Gallery, Macomb, IL.

A large comb decorates this woman's hairstyle. A large sausage curl drapes over one shoulder. Like the woman in the previous image, this woman wears a mantilla wrapped around her head.

Unidentified woman, late 1860s or early 1870s.

This older woman wears a bonnet that appears to have been made at home. It could have been crocheted. Small loops and leaves decorate this piece. Women's magazines often included instructions for making items like this.

Unidentified woman, 1870s.

A small flat hat, achieves height through the addition of an excess of trim—lace, tulle, and greenery. Her long hair is worn gathered at the crown under the hat, then long down the back. The photographer's studio props of rustic fence, leaves, and backdrop makes it difficult for a viewer to concentrate on the subject.

Unidentified couple, 1870s.

The small hat that rests atop this young woman's head features a striped edging. Her companion is hatless.

Unidentified group portrait, circa 1875.

The woman on the left wears her hair wrapped in a scarf with a small round hat on the top. The summer straw hat worn by the woman on the right has a wavy brim, flowers on the crown, and one side turned up. The man has placed his soft work hat on his lap. The woman on the left wears a checked cotton fabric dress, while the woman on the right wears a dress in a solid color. The photographer's backdrop depicts an outdoor scene with trees and a lake.

Unidentified women, early 1870s.

In the early 1870s, plenty of trim added height to small hats that were worn on top of elaborately coiffed hair. Feathers and ribbons decorate the crowns of these hats. The women on the right and left carry fur muffs and all of these subjects appear to be dressed for winter.

Unidentified man, early 1870s.

This man wears a soft cloth work cap with a wide bill and a peaked crown. The heavy coat worn over his jacket, tie wrapped under his collar, and a pair of striped fabric pants complete this outfit. The photographer posed him in a fringed chair.

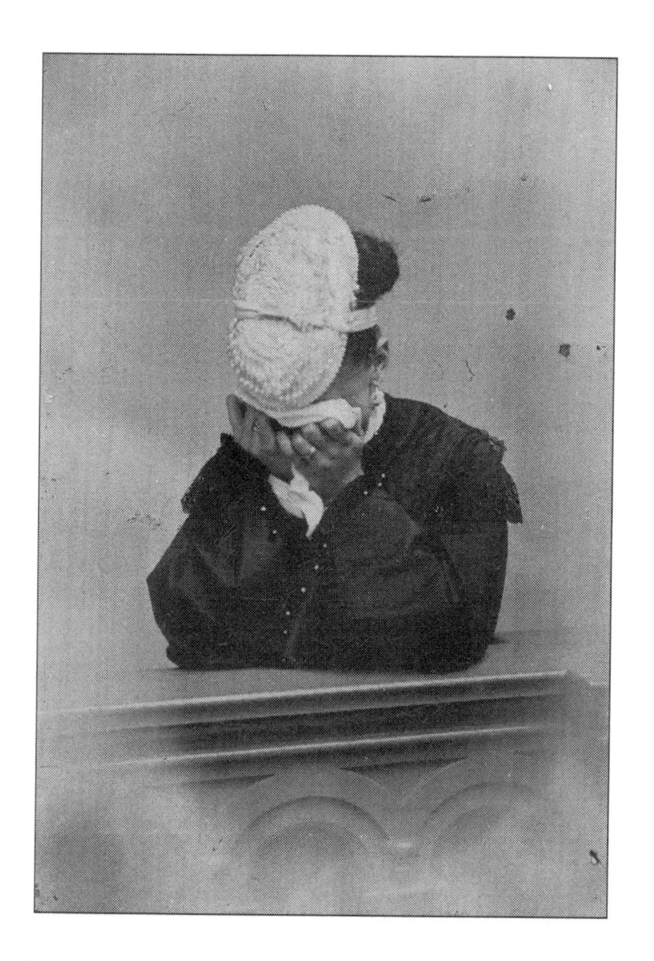

Unidentified woman, 1870s.

This unusual tintype seems to depict a woman weeping. The angle of this portrait provides a wonderful view of the top of her small straw hat as well as the band that wraps around her hair and ties at the top of her head, holding the headwear in place.

Unidentified woman, early 1870s.

Long hair trails down this woman's back while her small-brimmed, high-crowned hat rests on her head. The crown appears to be wrapped in ribbon while a single sprig of greenery emerges from one side. She wears drop earrings and a wool cape.

Unidentified woman, 1870s.

Similar to the hats depicted earlier in this chapter, this woman's headwear features a wide band of ribbon or tulle wrapped around the crown of her hat and hair. She wears a velvet-collared jacket over her dress. The photographer posed her pressing her hand on a paisley cloth covered table.

Unidentified young women, circa 1876.

The woman on the left wears a small hat with a medium-size crown. The velvet wrapped around the hat drops in a long wide swath down her back. Her friend wears a lovely straw hat with a ribbon trim. A small group of spring flowers decorates the top. The brim in the back is turned up. Gloves were a common accessory for women.

Unidentified young woman, 1870s.

According to the Library of Congress cataloging record, this woman wears a hat that is sometimes called "a flower pot" hat, a name that is reminiscent of its shape. Her lovely striped cotton dress and light-colored hat suggest this picture was taken in warmer months. The bustle is barely visible behind the arm on the left. The photographer's studio used a fringed chair instead of a table or a brace.

This photo might show John DeLany (b:1831) and sisters Luisa (b:1827), Caroline (b:1827), Betsy (b:1836), and Sarah (b:1840), or John's children, William (b:1853), Alice (b:1855), Ella (b:1857) Laura (b:1861), and Dorothy (b: 1867).

The woman on the right and the girl in front of her wear small top hats with front trim. The hat on the girl in the back has an upturned back brim. The man wears a simple soft hat with a wide brim. This photograph was taken overseas.

Unidentified man, 1870s.

This bright-eyed young man posed sitting in a fringed chair. On his head is a silk top hat with a very wide band. Note the narrow piping on the edge of his jacket lapel.

1880-1890

In the 1860s, Americans puzzled over English headgear, but in the 1880s, an English traveler had several comments to make about American hats. "As a general rule, it may be accepted that hats are made only for white men, and that the supplementary classes wear them after they have been thrown away."[40] By supplementary, he meant immigrants and African Americans. In a related article, a reporter asked "Where do the hats go?" This is a great question when we consider how hundreds of new styles became available each season. Many were sold at a discount; others were shipped to Southern dealers.[41]

The average man wore hats and so did the wealthy, but prominent individuals were known for their choice of head gear. President Chester Arthur wore a tall silk top hat, while presidential hopeful James Blaine preferred a black slouch hat "that he wore pulled down so low on his face it nearly touches his nose."[42] It was reported that President Arthur's hat was the only one of its kind in Washington. United States Attorney General Benjamin Brewster (1881-1885) had his white silk hats made in Philadelphia. Throughout the 1880s, low-crowned felt derbys with upturned brims were worn by younger men. According to Joan Severa, in *Dressed for the Photographer: Ordinary Americans and Fashion 1840-1900*, soft felt hats in gray and beige were common as were caps and the high-crowned hat known as the homburg.[43]

Colored straw hats made an appearance in the early 1880s as did wide Alsatian ribbons that appeared on large sailor hats.[44] In this decade, hats made from Mackinaw straw were the rage with milliners who also made black straw hats in various shapes. In both instances, these hats featured a band of bright color.

The Most Fashionable Braids for the Season of 1881. Examples from the Medway straw hat factory.

Panama hats, manufactured in Veraguas and Western Panama, were available in the U.S and the West Indies, but couldn't be imported into Europe. The cost of these hats varied greatly, from $2 to $150. When these durable hats got dirty, they could be easily cleaned using a mix of lime juice, soap, and water. [45]

Women's hats were made from a plush fabric. Often, the fabric, like corduroy or velvet, had a nap. Hats were plain, stripped, or spotted. In this period, turbans and walking hats made of felt also came into fashion. All sorts of shapes were common, ranging from poke bonnets to wide-brimmed Gainsborough's, named after the hats worn in portraits by painter Thomas Gainsborough. Bonnets were generally made in the **capote** style in many sizes. Women's hats, like those worn by men, featured high crowns with flat brims. Trims consisted of fake birds, bows, huge feathers, and flowers. According to Severa, there was knit headgear for women such as hoods, bonnets or "fascinators.[46]" Conquistador-style hats, fedora shaped straw hats, and practical shade hats with large brims that shielded faces all made an appearance in this decade.

An article in the *Huntsville Gazette* offered advice for women on a limited budget. The writer advised that those with few funds start with a hat. Wardrobe basics included a round black felt hat trimmed with a wide ribbon. These hats could be had for the cost of $1.00, were worn in all sorts of weather, and according to the article, generally lasted two years. For the summer, a white straw hat was a must for women. [47]

Hats and Bonnets in Great Variety

J.C. Johnson, importer of fine French millinery, is now offering special bargains in felt hats, bonnets and other goods in order to clear the store for Holiday stock. Fine felt hats in black and colors are reduced from $1.75 to 48 cents and from $1.25 to 25 cents. Velvet and plush hats and bonnets which formerly sold for $4 and $5, are now selling for $1.25, and fancy feathers, wings and birds are reduced in the same proportion. A table in the store is devoted to Majolica jardinières; faience vases and gilt baskets are filled with roses, carnations and other flowers, or with natural looking grapes, oranges, apples, and other fruits. Pansy baskets of purple and gold blossoms, with smilax, are fine copies of natural flowers and leaves.[48]

—*New York Herald-Tribune,* December 8, 1883.

How Plug Hats are Made

To make the silk stove-pipe hats, a large square of muslin is dipped into shellac, wrung out and then stretched over a wooden frame to dry. After drying it is cut up into sizes and shapes suitable for the various parts of the hat. Some pieces are cut on the bias for the crowns of hats, others are stiffened particularly for the brims, while the muslin for the central cylinders, which are the sides, is cut into oblong squares. The material for a dozen of these hats is then given to a workman who draws the frame of the hat together around the block and fastens it by means of a hot iron. The shell of the hat, as it is called, is then varnished and dried making it stiff and then the silk plush is put on, a man ironing it to the shellac-covered shell and sponging it with every stroke of the iron. Girls sew in the crown and the brim after the sides of the shell have been fastened and then the seams are gone over with a hot iron, which conceals all traces of them. The brim is then curled, as in the case of the felt article, and then the hat goes away to the luering machine, where polish brushes, revolving rapidly give it a high polish. [49]

—*Grand Forks Herald,* November 14, 1885.

What Hats Young Men May Wear

Dress hats for spring are of pearl gray cassimere, with a bell crown five and a half inches high, and round curved English brim that is nearly two inches wide. The felt hat for business and general wear is an English Derby larger than those lately worn; the crown is five and one-fourth inches high, and the rolled brim is two inches and an eighth in width. Cocoa brown is the stylish color, and there are navy blue and English green Derbys imported to match suits. American Derby hats have more tapering crows and are not so high as the English Shapes; they come in pearl color, black and brown. Traveling hats made in London are of cheviots in small checks or with mixed grounds, made with gores that curve to form a Derby crown; they are soft and have shapely rolled brims that are also soft, so that the hat can be put in the pocket or crushed without harm. Lawn tennis hats of soft felt, with low crowns and brims rolled all around, are shown in red, white, or blue felts, and there are larger hats of red moiré figured felt for ladies to wear when playing tennis—Harpers Bazar [*sic*].[50]

—*Daily Inter Ocean,* June 3, 1882.

Advertisement for Horsman's Celebrated Lawn Tennis equipment, Charles Hart Lith., circa 1882.

In the 1880s, people wore hats while playing sports. For tennis, soft caps were favored. In this ad, men wore sportswear designed for playing tennis, but the women wore form-fitting dresses and brimmed hats.

Unidentified woman, 1880s, W. Wright.

This large hat with a high crown and small brim was decorated with ribbon and flowers. The woman posed by resting on a rolled back-upholstered piece of studio furniture. She's holding one glove while still wearing the other. The draped fabric on the front of her skirt connects to a bustle.

According to Elizabeth Handler, the owner of this picture, the image likely depicts members of her family in either Chicago or Pittsburgh and dates to the 1870s.

Both men both wear felt hats. The hat on the left has a rounded crown and a flat brim in the style known as a "wide-awake." The hat on the right shows a wide band of ribbon on the crown. It is not unusual to see family members posed with a hand resting on their companion's shoulder.

Unidentified woman, 1880s, Geo. Cooper, Hull.

This lace capote-style bonnet was very fashionable for older women in the late 1880s. A capote is a close-fitting hat that resembles a cap. The woman's dress collar is a tiny lace band. She has fastened her neck scarf with a brooch.

Unidentified tintype, 1880s.

Here are three different styles of hats for young women—a wide-brimmed Gainsborough, a wide sun hat, and a straw boater with an upturned brim and a trailing ribbon. Dad wears a short-crowned, small-brimmed work hat. The wide lace collars shown here were very popular in the 1880s.

Unidentified man, 1880s.

This style of high-crowned derby/bowler hat was extremely popular in the 1880s. The hat in this photo has a medium size crown. The man wears a striped fabric overcoat over his suit. Full facial hair was commonplace in this decade.

Unidentified member of the Hahn or Hopp family, 1880s.

This wide-brimmed hat is another example of a Gainsborough. This studio features a rudimentary sketch as a backdrop, complete with a fence and a plaster rock.

Unidentified young woman, 1880s. Warren, Boston, MA.

In the 1880s, some women decorated their hair with large ribbons. Front curls were worn either frizzy or pasted to the forehead with hair products. This woman wears a simple everyday dress accented with a bar pin in the shape of a key.

Unidentified couple, 1880s.

This woman wears a high-peaked capote bonnet decorated with lace and trim. Her companion wears holds a bowler hat. Her dress features a bustle (just visible on right) and a draped skirt. The photographer's backdrop is interesting. Note the stairs painted into the scene behind the woman.

Unidentified woman, mid-1880s, Henshel, Chicago, IL.

In the mid-1880s, tall round hats with large front decorations were quite common. In this case, the straw hat has a large ribbon flower on the crown. The woman's dress features the large bustles that were common in the 1880s. Many women posed in profile to show off the shape of those bustles.

Unidentified woman, mid-1880s.

Here another woman wears a similarly styled hat. In this case, the hat is accented by a velvet brim and large oversize flowers on the front.

Unidentified woman, 1880s, Vickery, Haverhill, MA.

This small hat has an upturned brim in the back and draped fabric and a stuffed bird on the front. The woman wears a neck scarf.

Unidentified woman, 1880s.

A velvet turban surrounds this woman's neatly styled hair. She is dressed for cooler weather in a velvet-collared coat with oversize buttons.

Unidentified couple in England, 1880s.

Hat styles in the United States and England bore similarities—bowler hats for men and wide-brimmed hats for women. Notice the backdrop which depicts the English countryside with a thatched-roof house. In the foreground, the couple poses by a faux fence. He holds an umbrella while the photographer has supplied her with a basket of flowers.

Unidentified woman, late 1880s.

The size of this woman's bustle is balanced by the large plumed feather atop this curved brimmed hat. She wears gloves. This woman is posed in front of a backdrop that depicts a body of water, possibly the ocean.

Unidentified woman, 1880s.

There are so many lovely details in this tintype. She wears a small felt topper decorated with ribbon and flowers. A light fabric cape covers her dress, and she carries a small pocketbook.

Two unidentified women in summer hats, 1880s.

The hats worn in this tintype must have attracted attention. On the left, the woman's flat brim hat resembles a flower garden covered in trim and accented by one large blossom towering over the arrangement. Her companion wears a hat with some curve and plenty of trim to add height. Interestingly, the photographer posed them next to a large floral arrangement.

Unidentified group of men, 1880s.

Two of the men in this tintype wear summer straw hats with wide ribbon bands, while their friends opted for high-crowned bowler hats. The man on the far right wears a light-colored hat with a curled brim, very high crown, and a wide band.

Unidentified woman, late 1880s.

This woman poses confidently for the camera with her fan held slightly open. On her head is a flat-brimmed hat with a floral arrangement on the crown. The photographer's studio bench sits in front of the backdrop of an outdoor scene. Her dress features a center placket of accent fabric.

Unidentified woman, 1880s.

The round toque style hat is lovely. It appears to be trimmed with gathered fabric and a ribbon. The woman wears a striped cotton dress with a draped overskirt.

Unidentified men, 1880s.

Felt could be molded into a variety of shapes. These soft-looking hats are a bit unusual in shape. The man on the right wears a hat with a peaked crown that matches the long shape of his face. The fringed chair continues to be used in studios. The painted backdrop adds architectural elements.

Unidentified man, 1880s.

This man wears his soft felt hat at a rakish angle. It has a wide band and a narrow flat brim. Though it is similar in shape to the earlier photo of the felt hats worn by two men, this hat appears to be of better quality. He wears a watch chain on the front of his vest.

Group of unidentified women, 1880s.

These five women appear to have stopped at the photo studio on their way home from work. Each wears an apron tied around her waist. The wide fichu collars were common in the 1880s. While their hats all feature medium width brims, each is decorated differently with flowers and ribbons. They are posed in front of a backdrop of a house.

Unidentified men, 1880s.

The short fitted jackets shown here likely date to the 1880s. The men's light-colored top hats could be studio props or could have been bought for a special occasion. A silk band trims the tall-crowned hat on the right.

Unidentified men, 1880s.

Soft felt hats varied in shape and style. In this image, two men wear dented crown hats while their companions wear hats with an unstructured crown. The man on the left, front, wears a hat with a rolled brim.

Unidentified woman, late 1880s.

This woman's flat-brimmed hat is overwhelmed by the large feathers on the crown. But this decoration is typical for the period. There is a small ribbon towards the front of the brim. Her dress is beautifully beaded as was common in the late 1880s.

Unidentified woman, late 1880s.

This style of hat is meant to be worn on the back of the head so that the underside of the ruched fabric brim can be seen. A broad ribbon decorates the crown. This woman wears a beaded scarf, a bar pin, and a small necklace. Her braided hair is worn in a bun at the base of her head.

Unidentified woman, 1880s, L. Alman, New York and Newport.

A high-crowned plush hat sits atop this woman's light-colored curls. Her hat decorations include feathers, botanicals, and ribbon. She smiles for the camera leaving the viewer to wonder, "What's so funny?"

Theatrical poster of brunette woman, circa 1892, Calvert Litho. Co.

This image depicts a woman in a hat with a ruched underside and a large crown. While the date of the poster is circa 1892, the style of hat suggests the 1880s.

Frontier Hats [51]

John B. **Stetson**, the son of a Philadelphia hat manufacturer, developed consumption and went west to recover. Supposedly, he showed his traveling companions how to make tents from felt and also constructed a sample hat from the same material.

After he returned to Philadelphia in 1865, Stetson invested $100 in tools and fur while launching the John B. Stetson Hat Company. Initially, he designed typical hats, but when they didn't sell, he returned to the hat style he'd designed on the frontier. He called it the "Boss of the Plains." The hat was similar in design to those worn by members of the United States Army and by some confederate troops. Wide-brimmed hats were also worn on plantations. [52]

Stetson's marketing methods contributed to the hat's success. He sent samples to vendors throughout the United States. He wore his hat everywhere, becoming a walking advertisement for his product. And he made sure that a gold leaf "Stetson" appeared on the inside of every authentic hat from his company.

Unidentified man in a Stetson, 1880s. Collection of the author.

Western folks appreciated the simple design. A Stetson's high crown kept a man's head warm and the hat's waterproof qualities kept a man dry. These hats were also functional. Wearers could use them to retrieve water from streams or lakes for washing or drinking. The Stetson gained the nickname "ten-gallon hat" even though it only held about a half-gallon. In 1882, the best quality Stetson hats sold for $3.50.[53]

In 1906, Stetson died a millionaire. His company went bankrupt in 1970, but today his hat designs are licensed to HATCO and other manufacturers.

While their husbands (and a few wives) donned these utilitarian hats, frontier women wore bonnets that resembled styles worn in the 1840s. They were fitted at the back of the head and extended a bit past the face. A piece of fabric called a curtain covered the neck in the back. This functional headwear, protected women's skin from damaging sunlight and provided some shade. In this period, fashionable women shied away from freckled, tan complexions. Any woman could make her own bonnet from simple cotton fabric.

Distinctly western clothing—levis, chaps, and loose-fitting dresses called "mother hubbard's" enabled men and women to work unencumbered by fashion. From the tops of their Stetson or bonnet-covered heads to their functional boots, these frontier men and women wore what the rest of the world would consider "American fashion."[54]

Woman in a cotton bonnet, circa 1880s. Tintype. She wears a typical front-buttoned dress from the 1880s period. The tintype frame in this design helps date the photo.

Unidentified man, 1880s.

The flattering hat choice is just the right size for this man's head and complements his tight-fitting jacket. Small hats with curved brims were popular during the 1880s. Some had shallow crowns like this one, while others had medium or high crowns.

Unidentified man, 1880s.

This man wears a very modern looking hat in the homburg style. It has a slightly curved brim and a dent in the crown.

Unidentified young woman, circa 1880, A.F. Salisbury, Pawtucket, RI.

A lovely off-the-face hat that features large ribbons at the back. It tilts away from the face to show off the bangs popular in the 1880s.

1890-1900

The wide sleeves of the 1890s were offset with a variety of hats from small bonnets that tied under the chin to asymmetrical hats manufactured in interesting shapes. Just like 1880s, tiny capote bonnets were generally worn by older women while younger women favored fedoras and toques (a round hat worn low on the forehead). Wider hats with pinched backs and big fronts, hats with curled-up brims, peaked hats, and round *hats* with vertical trim on either side or at center, front, and back were all worn in this decade. Small platter-shaped hats had vertically wired trim of flowers, ribbons, feathers, wings, bows, and laces.

If there was any doubt that the 1890s woman loved hats, just consider the inventory when the G. Bernheimer, Bros and Co. store opened. The owners stocked over 800 hats with a wide variety of trims all from Paris. The display took up seventy square feet.[55] New offerings at department stores put even the most stylish hats, caps, and bonnets within the reach of the average woman.

People continued to don hats when playing sports. For instance, bicyclists wore small caps or tams. Anyone could look like a yachtsman in a straw sailor style hat.

The size of these irregularly-shaped hats sparked newspaper articles criticizing the trend. Women didn't remove their hats at events, which obscured the view of audience members trying to see the latest play or moving picture. The fashion led New York legislators to introduce a bill to require women to take off their big hats in the theater. (It didn't pass.)[56]

Men's hats were also produced in standard shapes ranging from stovepipe top hats for the wealthy to everyday derbys and stiffened bowlers. There were soft felt slouch hats in gray or black, stocking caps, and soft caps. After the Spanish-American War and the Philippine War—both conflicts with Spain—Panama straw hats returned to popularity.[57]

In the early 1890s, hats were trimmed with crushed fabric, flowers, or feathers. According to Severa, some of these hats were known as 'settin hens' because of the fluffed material at the back. At the end of decade, toques and felt hats remained in vogue and were often decorated with flowers for spring. Velvet was the fabric for theater hats. All styles continued to be set by what was worn in Paris.[58] Odd-shaped hats look even stranger when paired with dresses that boasted large sleeves in this decade.

Large hats with extensive brims and overly large trim were part of the 1895 summer season. That same year, vividly-colored hats were the fashion, but by 1896, hat colors were more subdued in shades of lilac and dahlia. Yellow was a favorite color.

The use of real stuffed birds as hat decorations incensed naturalists. In 1896, Harriet Hemenway and Minna Hall formed the Massachusetts Audubon Society in part due to the large number of birds being killed for decorative purposes. There was a general sense that nature was being threatened by man's carelessness.

In the 1890s, New York was considered the center of the hat industry. Factories had representatives in the city. The numbers are fascinating. Forty factories in the U.S. made all the straw hats, while thirty factories produced wool hats. Samples were on display in factory offices where wholesalers came to choose the next season's hats.[59] But New York did not have a lock on the market, factories based in Danbury, Connecticut made 6 million hats in 1890.

Why Wear Hats?

We Cling to a Custom that is
Neither Becoming Nor Health Giving

Why do both men and women persist in wearing hats? Asks Pearson's Magazine. There are three reasons why we should wear clothes. We may wear them for the sake of decency; for the sake of warmth; or for the sake of display. None of these reasons applies to the wearing of hats. Of course, there are head-coverings that are warm, such as the Icelander's sealskin hood or the fisherman's toque; but, as a rule, there is no real warmth in the hat of either sex. When a woman pins a slight structure of straw and artificial flowers on the top of her hair, she never for an instant imagines that the thing will keep her from taking cold. The masculine top hat is certainly warm on a hot day, but it is very far from warm in cold weather.

Neither are hats worn for the purpose of display. Doubtless there are times when women make the hat the occasion of displaying their fondness for dead birds, muslin flowers, and other beautiful objects, but this is only when fashion has decreed that big hats shall be worn. At other times the female hat is so microscopically small that it could not be successfully used for displaying anything. As for men's hats they never display anything except the atrocious taste which makes them fashionable. Why then, in the name of all that is sensible, do men and women wear hats?[60]

—Philadelphia Inquirer, October 27, 1899

This fashion plate shows three bust portraits of Jane Harding, Baronne de Carlsberg, and Suzanne, actresses at the Gymnase Theater, Paris, wearing hats designed in the Paris establishment of Madame Carlier. The image appeared in the *Millinery*, a magazine for the trade February, 1897.

Unidentified-woman, 1890s.

Her irregularly shaped hat features an enormous group of feathers that add height and width to her head wear.

Unidentified women, mid to late 1890s.

These women wear blouses with the leg of mutton sleeves that were so popular in the mid to late 1890s. Wide belts encircled their small waists. Their high collars look uncomfortable. Both wear hats trimmed with flowers and ribbons. On the right, the woman's hat has a wavy brim, while her friend wears a hat with an extended front brim.

Unidentified woman, late 1890s.

This woman is dressed for winter. Her heavy houndstooth plaid fabric coat is accessorized with a fur scarf, a muff to keep her hands warm, and a fur round toque hat.

Unidentified women, circa 1900.

To the contemporary viewer, these tiny crowned straw hats look silly, but in the late 1890s, they were the perfect accessory for a summer outfit. Both hats in this picture are trimmed with a wide silk band. One appears to be a light-colored straw while the other is dyed.

Hannah nee Cursley SAFFORD (1829-1908) born and died in Bedfordshire, England.

She had eight children, only one of whom, Newman (a.k.a Harry) Safford, emigrated to the U.S. in 1885, via Toronto. Following her husband's death, Hannah Safford operated a "public house" at 18 Newnham Street, Bedford.

Her granddaughter stated in a letter written in 1983: "I used to visit Bedford with my mother, and I only saw my grandmother several times. My mother used to say she was 'a lady bred and born'."Cursley like others of her age, chose to wear a close-fitting capote bonnet. It is trimmed in lace and ribbon.

Unidentified women, late 1890s

The woman on the left wears a hat with a wide brim and a concave crown accented by a feather. On the right, her friend wears a round toque topped by a large stuffed bird.

Unidentified young woman, circa 1900.

Large feathers adorn this woman's hat along with a silk band and buckle. Around her neck, she wears a feather boa.

Unidentified young woman, circa 1900.

This improbably-designed hat looks precariously perched on this woman's head. Large feathers stick out of the kidney-shaped crown.

Unidentified woman, late 1890s.

A reinforced ribbon sticks out of the top of this woman's small brimless straw hat. She wears a short coat with leg of mutton sleeves. A rose corsage decorates the jacket. In her hand, she carries a small clutch bag.

Unidentified woman, late 1890s.

Similar in shape to the hat shown in the previous photo, this woman's topper is clearly made for winter. It has a wavy shape and is trimmed with patterned ribbons and a feather. She's dressed for cold weather in a fur-trimmed short jacket and muff.

Unidentified woman, circa 1900.

A large bow is the focal point in this odd-shaped hat. Feathers of various colors grace the sides. It's a tiny hat compared to the size of her head.

Unidentified woman, circa 1900.

Multiple feathers and ribbons extend from the surface of this flat-topped winter hat. The combination of the large sleeves on her cloak and the size of her hat dwarf her face.

Unidentified woman, 1893, Rombaugh, Montgomery City, MO.

This young woman wears a straw hat with trailing ribbons and tall reinforced ribbons on top. Her dress features a wide-wrapped waist and a ruffled yoke.

Arthur S. Merritt (30 years old in photo) with his wife Emma, December 2, 1895, Lynn, MA.

These shop owners posed in front of their establishment. In the windows are caps and gloves. Their sign advertises that they have a large variety of items at the lowest prices. A string of gloves hangs over the doorway.

Unidentified members of the Hahn or Hoppe family, late 1890s.

The daughter wears a graduation-style hat, while her mother wears a style of hat known as a Pinchback Watteau. The mother's hat is decorated with feathers and ribbons, typical adornment on winter head wear.

Unidentified woman, late 1890s.

A gorgeous spring hat graces the head of this young woman. The tradition of Easter bonnets was related to the wealthy families of New York. This woman's hat is similar to a flat plate with an enormous bow decorating the top.

Unidentified model holding a sign for Laing's Palace Millinery, late 1890s, Doan, Brookfield, MO.

William Laing of Brookfield, Missouri used this photograph to advertise his millinery business. A woman poses with her back to the camera, head turned to the right to profile the elaborate creation on her head. Feathers rise off her hat at the top and the back. Rosettes decorate the side facing the camera.

Laing immigrated to the United States in 1868 from Canada. In the 1900 census, he was 56 living with his 49 year old wife.[61]

GLOSSARY

Bowler	Dome-shaped crown in various heights with a curled brim. Also called a derby.
Boater	Flat-brimmed and flat-crowned straw hat.
Capote	Small cap-like hat that fit the head.
Day cap	Muslin cap worn by married women while they were indoors.
Eton cap	Style of cap worn by the boys at the English school, Eton.
Gainsborough	Simple wide-brimmed hat.
Panama hat	Straw hat originally made in Ecuador from toquilla palm.
Pillbox hat	Cylindrical hat.
Porkpie hat	Flat hat with a short crown and rolled brim.
Poke bonnet	Hat that resembled a coal scuttle.
Snood	Type of hairnet.
Stetson	High-crowned waterproof hat.
Stovepipe	Tall hat with flat sides.
Toque	Hat with no brim.
Trilby	Named after a character in the 1895 play by George du Maurier. It's a soft felt hat with a dented brim.
Turban	Hat which is wrapped around the head.
Wide-Awake	Flat-crowned hat with wide brim.

BIBLIOGRAPHY

"A Dangerous Bonnet." *Albany Evening Journal*. April 17, 1856.

Advertisement. *Muskegon Chronicle*. June 2, 1882.

Allison-Antrim Museum. Accessed August 28, 2010. [www.greencastle museum.org].

"American Hats." *Springfield Republican*. September 13, 1882.

Baseball Hall of Fame. "Dressed to the Nines—Parts of the Uniform." Accessed October 5, 2011. [http://exhibits.baseballhalloffame.org/dressed_to_the_nines/caps.htm].

"Betsy Baker's Bonnet." *Lowell Daily Citizen and News*. August 13, 1859.

"Bonnets and Hats." *Huntsville Gazette*. July 16, 1881.

Boston Evening Transcript. April 10, 1846.

Boston Evening Transcript. December 28, 1847.

Chrisp, Peter. *History of Fashion and Costume: The Victorian Age*, vol. 6 New York: Facts On File, 2005.

"Colors in Ladies' Dresses." *New Hampshire Patriot*. May 12, 1852.

"Cost of Last Sunday's Parade." *Worcester Daily Spy*. April 25, 1897.

Cumming, Valerie, C. W. Cunnington, and P.E. Cunnington. *The Dictionary of Fashion History*. New York: Oxford, 2010.

"Eight Hundred Beauties, All Different, but All in the Mode." *Kansas City Times*. September 26, 1894.

"Fashions in Millinery." *New York Herald*. October 20, 1879.

"Fremont Hats." *Wisconsin Free Democrat*. October 22, 1856.

"Great Men's Hats: The Distinctive Styles of the Headgear of Prominent Politicians." *San Francisco Bulletin*. September 13, 1884.

Hall, Lee. *Common Threads: A Parade of American Clothing.* Boston: Little, Brown and Company, 1992.

"Hats." *Plain Dealer (Cleveland).* April 29, 1851.

"Hats." *Daily Democratic State Journal.* June 27, 1856.

"How to dress for a photograph." *New Orleans Times.* April 9, 1865.

"How to Make a Fashionable Bonnet." *Barre Patriot* (Massachusetts). August 4,1854.

"Hats and Bonnets in Great Variety." *New York Herald-Tribune.* December 8, 1883.

"How Plug Hats are Made." *Grand Forks Herald.* November 14,1885.

Johnson, Barbara. *Antique and Vintage Fashions, 1745-1979: A Collector's Guide.* Paducah, Kentucky: Collector Books, 2009.

Kasal, Mark and Don Moore. *A Guide to U.S. Army Dress Helmets, 1872-1904.* North Cape Publications, 2000.

Kennett, Frances. *Collectors Book of Fashion.* New York: Crown, 1984.

"Ladies' New Straw Hats." *Macon Telegraph.* March 3, 1882.

"Jackets, Gloves, and Hats." *Daily Inter Ocean.* July 21, 1882.

Langley, Susan. *Vintage Hats & Bonnets, 1770-1970.* Paducah, Kentucky: Collector Books, 1998.

Macon Telegraph. June 11, 1865.

"Men's Hats for the Year." Kansas City Times. February 15, 1891.

Morning News (New London). May 5, 1846.

New Hampshire Patriot. August 18, 1847.

"New Styles of Bonnet." *St. Paul Daily Pioneer.* February 13, 1855.

Nuttall, Kelly. "The History of Stetson Hats." Accessed October 13, 2010. [www.ehow.com].

Ohio Statesman. March 1, 1842.

Ortner, Jessica. *Practical Millinery.* London: Whittaker & Co, 1897.

"Panama Hats." *Kalamazoo Gazette.* September 22, 1880.

"Panama Hats in Favor." *Daily Herald.* September 17, 1899.

Philadelphia Inquirer. October 27, 1899.

"Please don't wear big hats." *New York Herald-Tribune.* January 26, 1895.

Severa, Joan L. *Dressed for the Photographer: Ordinary Americans and Fashion, 1840-1900.* Kent, OH: Kent State University Press, 1995.

———. *My Likeness Taken: Daguerreian Portraits in America.* Kent, OH: Kent State University Press, 2005.

Shephard, Norma. *1,000 Hats.* Atglen, PA: Schiffer, 2006.

"Shocking Bad Hats" of the Prince of Wales Suite. *San Franciscan Bulletin.* November 21, 1860.

Sichel, Marion. *The Victorians.* Boston: Plays Inc., 1978.

"Spring Bonnets: Radical Changes in the Head Dresses of the Fair." *New York Herald.* March 23, 1879.

Steele, Philip. *The Nineteenth Century: History of Fashion and Costume.* New York: Facts on File, 2005.

"Secession Bonnet." *Philadelphia Inquirer.* December 25, 1860.

Sullivan, Edmund B. *Collecting Political Memorabilia.* Hanover, MA: Christopher Publishing House, 1991.

"Summer Bonnets." *Plain Dealer.* May 26, 1859.

"Talk on Hats and Bonnets." *New York Herald-Tribune.* January 18, 1898.

"The Distinctive Styles of the Headgear of Prominent Politicians." *San Francisco Bulletin.* September 13, 1884.

"The Fashions: Spring Opening Days." *New York Herald-Tribune.* March 27, 1877.

"The Fall Style of Bonnets." *The Sun.* September 10, 1857.

"The Love Knot." *New York Herald-Tribune.* January 12, 1858.

"The New Hat and Bonnet." *Galveston Weekly News.* October 15, 1877.

"The Panama Hat Plant." *Galveston Weekly News.* July 23, 1877.

The Sun (Massachusetts). May 31, 1856.

"The Union Straw Works at Foxborough. How Bonnets are Made." *Boston Daily Advertiser.* November 23, 1866.

Weekly Eagle (Vermont). June 15, 1848.

Weekly Wisconsin Patriot. April 19, 1856.

"What Hats Young Men May Wear." *Daily Inter Ocean.* June 3, 1882.

"Where do the hats go?" *Grand Forks Herald.* January 7, 1883.

White, Richard Grant. *England Without and Within.* Boston: Houghton Mifflin, 1881.

"Why Wear Hats." *Philadelphia Inquirer.* October 27, 1899.

MAGAZINES AND WEBSITES

Demorest's.

Frank Leslie's Gazette.

Godey's Lady's Book.

Journal Des Demoiselles.

Library of Congress.

Millinery.

Peterson's Magazine.

Wikipedia: The Free Encyclopedia.

CREDITS

Photo credits are listed by page number.

2 *Journal des Demoiselles*, 1840s.

4 Library of Congress, Dag. No. 060.

5 Library of Congress, Brady-Handy Collection, Dag. No. 518x.

6 *Godey's Lady's Book,* February, 1841, 49.

7 *Godey's Lady's Book*, December, 1849, 454.

8 *Godey's Lady's Book*, December 1849, 462.

9 Collection of the author.

10 Library of Congress, Madame Petit's French Millinery, Dress & Flower Making Establishment..

11 Collection of the author.

12 Library of Congress Dag. No. 1414.

15 Courtesy of Medway Historical Society.

18 Collection of the author.

19 Library of Congress, Dag. No. 1241.

20 Collection of the author.

21 Collection of the author.

22 Collection of the author.

23 Collection of the author

24 Collection of the author.

25 Library of Congress, Dag. No. 393.

26 Library of Congress, unprocessed in PR13 CN 1979:169.

27 Library of Congress, Charles E. Feinberg Walt Whitman collection.

28 Library of Congress, Dag. No. 1242.

29 Library of Congress, Dag. No. 1279.

30 Library of Congress, Part of the Gilbert H. Grosvenor Collection of Photographs of the Alexander Graham Bell Family. Dag. No. 1135.

31 Library of Congress, Dag. No. 1046A.

32 Library of Congress, Dag. No. 1365.

33 Collection of the author.

34 Library of Congress, Dag. No. 215.

35 Library of Congress, LC-USZC4-3888, Dag. No. 330.

37 Library of Congress, Lot 7881.

39 Courtesy of Footnote Maven.

40 Collection of Jane Schwerdtfeger.

41 Collection of Jane Schwerdtfeger.

42 Collection of Jane Schwerdtfeger.

43 Collection of Phil Storey.

44 Courtesy of Elizabeth Handler.

45 *Godey's Lady's Book*, October, 1864, 291, 365.

46 Collection of Jane Schwerdtfeger.

47 Collection of the author.

48 Library of Congress, LOT 11162, No. 29.

49 Collection of the author.

50 Library of Congress, LOT 14022, No. 45.

51 Collection of the author.

52 Collection of the author.

53 Courtesy of Sandy Willis.

54 Collection of the author.

55 Collection of the author.

56 Library of Congress, AMB/TIN 2713.

57 Library of Congress, PGA-Rogers-Philip Hill.

58 Collection of the author.

59 Collection of the author.

60 Collection of Jane Schwerdtfeger.

61 *Godey's Lady's Book*, January, 1863, 19.

62 Collection of Jane Schwerdtfeger.

63 Library of Congress, Liljenquist Family Collection, AMB/TIN No. 2080.

64 Library of Congress, Lijenquist Family Collection, AMB/TIN No. 2573.

65 Collection of the author.

66 Collection of the author.

67 Collection of the author.

68 Collection of the author.

69 Collection of the author.

70 Collection of the author.

74 Collection of Phil Storey.

75 *Journal Des Demoiselles*, n.d.

76 Collection of the author.

77 Collection of Phil Storey.

78 Library of Congress, Lot 13656 No. 2.

79 Courtesy of Maridee Alexander.

80 Collection of the author.

81 Collection of Jane Schwerdtfeger.

82 Collection of the author.

83 Collection of Jane Schwerdtfeger.

84 Collection of the author.

85 Collection of the author.

86 Collection of the author.

87 Collection of the author.

88 Collection of the author.

89 Collection of the author.

90 Collection of the author.

91 Collection of the author.

92 Collection of the author.

93 Collection of the author.

94 Collection of the author.

95 Collection of the author.

96 Collection of the author.

97 Collection of the author.

98 Library of Congress, Lot 5754-F, No. 1.

99 Courtesy of Jean Sebasta.

100 Collection of Phil Storey

102 Courtesy of Medway Historical Society

105 Library of Congress. "Horsman's Celebrated Lawn Tennis," Charles Hart, lith., c. 1882.

106 Collection of the author.

107 Courtesy of Elizabeth Handler.

108 Collection of the author.

109 Collection of the author.

110 Collection of the author.

111 Courtesy of Sandy Willis.

112 Collection of the author.

113 Collection of the author.

114 Collection of Jane Schwerdtfeger.

115 Collection of the author.

116 Collection of the author.

117 Collection of Jane Schwerdtfeger.

118 Collection of the author.

119 Collection of the author.

120 Collection of the author.

121 Collection of the author.

122 Collection of the author.

123 Collection of the author.

124 Library of Congress, Unprocessed in PR 13 CN 1999:022, No. 1.

125 Collection of Phil Storey.

126 Collection of Phil Storey.

127 Collection of the author.

128 Collection of Phil Storey.

129 Collection of the author.

130 Collection of the author.

131 Collection of the author.

132 Collection of the author.

133 Library of Congress, POS-TH-STO, No. 11.

134 Collection of the author.

135 Collection of the author.

136 Collection of the author.

137 Collection of the author.

138 Collection of the author.

142 Library of Congress, "The Millinery Trade Review," February 1897. New York: Millinery Associates, Inc. pl 4.

143 Library of Congress, Lot 11930, No. 81. In album: Types of American Negroes, Compiled and prepared by W.E. B. Du Bois, V. 1 No. 81 P.

144 Collection of the author.

145 Collection of the author

146 Collection of the author.

147 Courtesy of Jennifer L. David.

148 Library of Congress, Lot 1193, Types of American Negroes, Compiled and prepared by W.E.B. Du Bois, V. 1, No. 100.

149 Library of Congress, Lot 1193, Types of American Negroes, Compiled and prepared by W.E.B. Du Bois, V. 1, No. 40.

150 Library of Congress, Lot 1193, Types of American Negroes, Compiled and prepared by W.E.B. Du Bois, V. 1, No. 89.

151 Collection of Jane Schwerdtfeger.

152 Collection of Jane Schwerdtfeger.

153 Collection of Jane Schwerdtfeger.

154 Collection of Jane Schwerdtfeger.

155 Courtesy of Gwen Prichard.

156 Courtesy of Footnote Maven.

157 Courtesy of Sandy Willis.

158 Collection of Jane Schwerdtfeger.

159 Collection of the author.

ENDNOTES

[1] *Philadelphia Inquirer*, October 27, 1899, 11. Courtesy of GenealogyBank.com.

[2] "Hats," *Daily Democratic State Journal*, June 27, 1856, 2. Courtesy of GenealogyBank.com.

[3] "How to dress for a photograph," *New Orleans Times*, April 9, 1865, 2. Courtesy of GenealogyBank.com.

[4] "Colors in Ladies' Dresses," *New Hampshire Patriot*, May 12, 1852, 4. Courtesy of GenealogyBank.com.

[5] Richard Grant White, *England Without and Within* (Boston: Houghton Mifflin, 1881) 55.

[6] "Dressed to the Nines—Parts of the Uniform," Baseball Hall of Fame, [http://exhibits.baseballhalloffame.org/dressed_to_the_nines/caps.htm], accessed October 5, 2011.

[7] "Cost of Last Sunday's Parade," *Worcester Daily Spy*, April 25, 1897, 13. Courtesy of GenealogyBank.com.

[8] Jessica Ortner, *Practical Millinery* (London: Whittaker & Co, 1897) 1.

[9] *New Hampshire Patriot*, August 18, 1847, 4. Courtesy of GenealogyBank.com.

[10] *Weekly Eagle* (Vermont), June 15, 1848, 4. Courtesy of GenealogyBank.com.

[11] *Morning News* (New London), May 5, 1846, 4. Courtesy of GenealogyBank.com.

[12] *Boston Evening Transcript,* April 10, 1846, 4. Courtesy of GenealogyBank.com.

[13] *Ohio Statesman*, March 1, 1842, 4. Courtesy of GenealogyBank.com.

[14] *Boston Evening Transcript*, December 28, 1847. Courtesy of Genealogy Bank.com.

[15] *Times-Picayune,* October 30, 1840, 2. Courtesy of GenealogyBank.com.

[16] *Godey's Lady's Book*, December, 1849, 462.

[17] *Weekly Wisconsin Patriot*, April 19, 1856, 3. Courtesy of GenealogyBank. com.

[18] *The Sun* (Massachusetts), May 31, 1856, 2. Courtesy of GenealogyBank. com.

[19] "The Union Straw Works at Foxborough. How Bonnets are Made," *Boston Daily Advertiser*, November 23, 1866, 1.

[20] "Betsy Baker's Bonnet," *Lowell Daily Citizen and News*, August 13, 1859, 2. Courtesy of GenealogyBank.com.

[21] "A Dangerous Bonnet," *Albany Evening Journal*, April 17, 1856, 2. Courtesy of GenealogyBank.com.

[22] "The Fall Style of Bonnets," The Sun, September 10, 1857, 2. Courtesy of GenealogyBank.com.

[23] "Hats," *Plain Dealer (Cleveland)*, April 29, 1851, 2. Courtesy of GenealogyBank.com.

[24] "Fremont Hats," *Wisconsin Free Democrat*, October 22, 1856, 3. Courtesy of GenealogyBank.com.

[25] "The Love Knot," *New York Herald-Tribune,* January 12, 1858, 2. Courtesy of GenealogyBank.com.

[26] "How to Make a Fashionable Bonnet," *Barre Patriot* (Massachusetts), August 4,1854, 1. Courtesy of GenealogyBank.com.

[27] "New Styles of Bonnet," *St. Paul Daily Pioneer,* February 13, 1855, 2. Courtesy of GenealogyBank.com

[28] "Summer Bonnets," *Plain Dealer,* May 26, 1859, 3. Courtesy of GenealogyBank.com.

[29] "Shocking Bad Hats" of the Prince of Wales Suite, *San Franciscan Bulletin*, November 21, 1860, 1.

[30] "Secession Bonnet," *Philadelphia Inquirer,* December 25, 1860, 4. Courtesy of GenealogyBank.com.

[31] *Macon Telegraph,* June 11, 1865, 4. Courtesy of GenealogyBank.com.

[32] Edmund B. Sullivan, *Collecting Political Americana* (Hanover, MA: Christopher Publishing House, 1991), 141-146.

[33] *Godey's Lady's Book,* January, 1863, 19.

[34] "The Fashions: Spring Opening Days," *New York Herald-Tribune*, March 27, 1877, 2. Courtesy of GenealogyBank.com.

[35] The Fashions: Spring Opening Days," *New York Herald-Tribune*, March 27, 1877, 2. Courtesy of GenealogyBank.com.

[36] "Fashions in Millinery," *New York Herald*, October 20, 1879, 8. Courtesy of GenealogyBank.com.

[37] "The Panama Hat Plant," *Galveston Weekly News*, July 23, 1877, 5. Courtesy of GenealogyBank.com.

[38] "The New Hat and Bonnet," *Galveston Weekly News,* October 15, 1877, 7. Courtesy of GenealogyBank.com.

[39] "Spring Bonnets: Radical Changes in the Head Dresses of the Fair," *New York Herald*, March 23, 1879, 9. Courtesy of GenealogyBank.com.

[40] "American Hats," *Springfield Republican*, September 13, 1882, 5. Courtesy of GenealogyBank.com.

[41] "Where do the hats go?" *Grand Forks Herald*, January 7, 1883, 2. Courtesy of GenealogyBank.com.

[42] "Great Men's Hats: The Distinctive Styles of the Headgear of Prominent Politicians," *San Francisco Bulletin*, September 13, 1884, 2. Courtesy of GenealogyBank.com.

[43] Joan Severa, *Dressed for the Photographer: Ordinary Americans and Fashion 1840-1900, (Kent, OH: Kent State University Press, 1995), 388.*

[44] "Ladies' New Straw Hats," *Macon Telegraph*, March 3, 1882, 2; "Jackets, Gloves, and Hats," *Daily Inter Ocean*, July 21, 1882, 5. Courtesy of GenealogyBank.com.

[45] "Panama Hats," *Kalamazoo Gazette*, September 22, 1880, 3. Courtesy of GenealogyBank.com.

[46] Severa, p. 386.

[47] "Bonnets and Hats," *Huntsville Gazette*, July 16, 1881, 4. Courtesy of GenealogyBank.com.

[48] "Hats and Bonnets in Great Variety," *New York Herald-Tribune,* December 8, 1883. Courtesy of GenealogyBank.com.

[49] "How Plug Hats are Made," *Grand Forks Herald,* November 14,1885, 3. Courtesy of GenealogyBank.com.

[50] "What Hats Young Men May Wear,"*Daily Inter Ocean,* June 3, 1882, 3. Courtesy of GenealogyBank.com.

[51] Maureen Taylor, "Out West: Hats on The Frontier," *Shades of the Departed,* shadesthemagazine-archive.blogspot.com, December 2010, 10-16.

[52] Kelly Nuttall, "The History of Stetson Hats," [www.ehow.com], accessed October 13, 2010.

[53] Advertisement, *Muskegon Chronicle,* June 2, 1882, 3. Courtesy of GenealogyBank.com.

[54] Lee Hall, *Common Threads: A Parade of American Clothing* (Boston: Little, Brown and Company, 1992, 93-114).

[55] "Eight Hundred Beauties, All Different, but All in the Mode," *Kansas City Times*, September 26, 1894, 2. Courtesy of GenealogyBank.com.

[56] "Please don't wear big hats," *New York Herald-Tribune,* January 26, 1895. Courtesy of GenealogyBank.com.

[57] "Panama Hats in Favor," *Daily Herald*, September 17, 1899, 10. Courtesy of GenealogyBank.com.

[58] "Talk on Hats and Bonnets" New York Herald-Tribune January 18, 1898, 5. Courtesy of GenealogyBank.com.

[59] "Men's Hats for the Year," Kansas City Times, February 15, 1891, 17. Courtesy of GenealogyBank.com.

[60] "Why Wear Hats," *Philadelphia Inquirer,* October 27, 1899, 11. Courtesy of GenealogyBank.com.

[61] 1900 U.S. census, Linn County, Missouri, pop. Sch., Ward 2 Brookfield, ED 68, p. 54 (stamped), dwelling 1203, family 6, William Laing.

Other books by Maureen Taylor

Available on www.maureentaylor.com

Fashionable Folks:
Hairstyles 1840-1900
$19.95

Finding the Civil War in
Your Family Album
$24.95

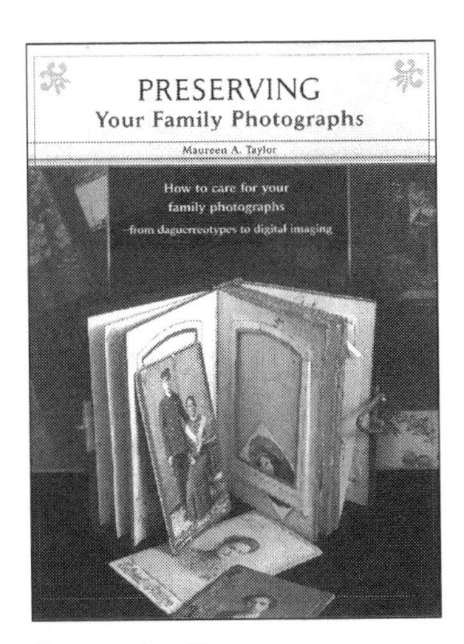

Preserving Your
Family Photographs
$24.95

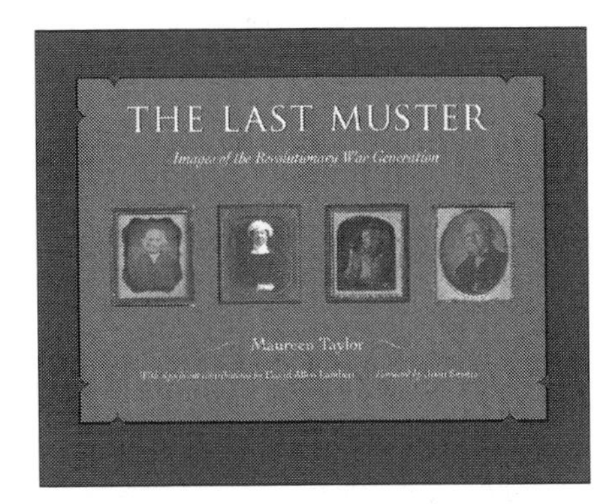

The Last Muster: Images of the
Revolutionary War Generation
$45.00

Need more photo identification tips and techniques? Sign up for Maureen's free e-newsletter on her website.

Got a photo preservation related question? Go to www.askmaureentaylor and register for her podcasts.

Made in the USA
Charleston, SC
28 June 2012